LITERATURE EVANGELISM

LITERATURE EVANGELISM

George Verwer

Contents

Introduction

When I was 14 I received through the post a copy of the Gospel of John, sent by a dear Christian lady who believed that God answers prayer and who believed in the power of the Gospel in printed form. For two years I read that little booklet regularly until, at an evangelistic meeting, I was 'born again, not of perishable seed, but of imperishable, through the living and enduring word of God' (1 Pet. 1:23).

The day following my conversion I began to evangelise with literature and personal testimony, and I have continued to do so ever since. During this time I have had many lessons to learn, and God has used many people and Christian organisations to teach me. I am also indebted to a multitude of Christian young people through whom God has taught me still more precious lessons. These young people, from many different countries, are involved in world evangelism, and are distributing tens of millions of pieces of Christian literature throughout much of the world. It is from their experiences that I have been able to gather the material for this book.

I first wrote this book 40 years ago. Since then it has gone out across the world in dozens of languages. Many things have changed in the intervening years, especially with the World Wide Web and e-mail. We now even have e-books! In one form or another, there are more people reading than ever before. With the world population almost doubling to now over six billion people, our task remains huge, and the need for a further revised edition of this book is great.

Above all that I have learned from other people, the greatest lesson has been one which God has taught me through His word and through His correcting hand. It is this: if there is to be victory in the Christian life and in the service of our Lord, it is absolutely essential that we keep our eyes constantly on the Saviour. If we set our eyes on the work and allow ourselves to get caught up in the activity of doing, we can expect only frustration. If we set our eyes on human beings and what they can do for us or we for them, we will receive only disappointment. Sooner or later we will find our hearts filled with unbelief because we will be seeking honour from other people rather than that which comes from God (John 5:44).

We can expect God's blessing when our eyes are fixed unwaveringly on Him. Even such good things as personal witnessing, literature evangelism, Bible teaching or preaching must be subordinated to our main goal which is God Himself. We must look continually to Jesus Christ. We must seek to know Him and to walk daily with Him. We must abide in Him. Because this has come to be of primary importance to me, it is my prayer that this book will only be read by those who know and obey Jesus Christ, and who want to honour Him with all that is within them.

This book is not exhaustive, for the subject is broad and I am still in the process of learning many things. I am, however, certain that anyone who takes the matter of literature evangelism seriously will find much in this book to equip them better for the work of confronting people with Christ.

I have often been guilty of challenging people to distribute literature without telling them how to do it. I pray that this book will help fill that gap and that many who have been challenged to do this work will, in these pages, find the practical information which will help them to reach people for Jesus Christ.

1

The Need for Christian Literature

When this book was revised in 1977 the world population had already doubled during the century to four billion. I wrote then that by the year 2000 it would be six billion – and that is now history. It is this population explosion which has caused Christian leaders to conclude that, if the entire world is ever to hear of Christ, the church must become totally involved in world evangelism. There is general agreement that one of the key ingredients in the fulfilling of this great responsibility is the increased use of literature. Christian literature, however, must more than ever be used in partnership with every other form of communication.

We have learned gradually over the years how literature becomes part of ministry to the whole person. We discovered in OM that our use of educational books, first in Nepal and then in a mammoth way on our ships, was to be a vital part of our ministry, and not just a means to an end. Now we find ourselves publishing health books for Afghan refugees and guides to help people understand and prevent HIV and AIDS.

This is not a new discovery. Benjamin Franklin once said, 'Give me 26 lead soldiers, and I will conquer the world.' He was speaking, of course, of the 26 letters of the English alphabet cast in printer's type. He knew the power of the printed page. So too did Martin Luther, who circulated hundreds of thousands of pamphlets throughout Europe on the eve of the Reformation. Karl Marx and Lenin recognised the power of literature, as do many of the cultist groups of today. The amazing growth of many of these groups is in close proportion to their zeal in the propagation of their literature. They have not underestimated the importance of those little lead soldiers.

Through the various Scripture publication and distribution agencies hundreds of millions of New Testaments, Bibles and Scripture portions are published and distributed each year. We thank God for all who are involved in the publication and translation of the Scriptures around the world, such as the United Bible Societies, the largest publishers of Bibles in the world, and Living Bibles International, who years ago merged with the International Bible Society and have translated and published modern, readable New Testaments and Bibles in over 600 languages. Wycliffe Bible Translators and others continue to translate the Bible into new languages, and they, with many others, have entered into tribal areas, sometimes risking their lives to put the Scriptures into the languages of the people. Many more languages have been discovered since I first wrote this book and so there are still about 3000 language groups in the world without Scripture.

We have proved, however, that having the Word of God in someone's language does not mean that the average person will ever have a copy. It is estimated that around 20 per cent of the world's population has never read or heard the Gospel in any form. There is much yet to be done!

What have we learned in the past 40 years in which literature ministry, and related ministries such as audio and video, have multiplied tenfold? I believe we have learned that God uses all these tools, but generally they are not enough. He needs people – people who will do the follow-up work and plant the living churches; people who will, in various ways, demonstrate God's grace and love in the midst of communities by being involved in every aspect of building the Kingdom.

In most of the major languages we now have all kinds of powerful materials. Sad to say, however, the distribution and use of the materials is low. Hundreds of millions, especially in what is now known as the 10/40 Window (the area of the world between latitudes 10° and 40° north of the equator, including North Africa, the Middle East and Asia), have never even had a Bible or Christian book in their hands. Hundreds of millions may have seen a Gospel TV presentation like the large ones Billy Graham did some years ago, but there are still hundreds of millions who have never seen one, especially in their own language.

A further question arises when we realise that a great part of all literature work and other media ministry is dedicated to the publication of books specifically for Christians. We understand, or course, the importance of materials to teach Christians, but we are struck nevertheless with the following rather unjust proportion: for every book written to present the way of salvation to the unconverted person, there are hundreds written for the benefit of the Christian.

Why this lack of balance? One of the reasons is that selling books to Christians is relatively easy compared with selling to those who are not believers. Christian books are usually not distributed through the secular market, but through church bookstalls, radio broadcast offers, Christian bookshops, and Christian book clubs. These are methods which lose most of their effectiveness with the person who is not a Christian and who does not generally seek our Christian books, although the Spirit of God has caused many individuals to do this.

When thinking of evangelism by means of literature, as we are doing in this book, it is primarily the non-Christian we want to reach. It is distribution to the unsaved which is the biggest bottleneck in the field of literature today, as it is also with other media.

Without a doubt the most effective means of getting Christian literature into the hands of the unsaved is by taking it to them. The evangelistic method of the apostle Paul was not so much 'You come and hear me' as 'I'll bring it to you.' He said, 'I have not hesitated to preach anything that would be helpful to you but have taught you publicly and from house to house' (Acts 20:20). Christians in radio, TV, and even now with web sites, have been coming up with more creative ways to get the Gospel to the non-Christian, but we still have a long way to go. We believe that every believer needs to be mobilised into action.

Paul was a great officer in the army of the Lord, a man of intellect and influence, but he never stopped being a foot soldier, knocking on doors to witness for his Lord. Yet today it is very difficult to find Christian men and women who are willing to go from house to house witnessing and distributing literature and sharing their faith. Satan is a master strategist. A

Christian leader once said to me, 'Eye-contact with the unconverted is something Satan will do everything to keep us from.' He delights in tying God's people into organisational knots, which keep production as the end in view and distract us from the question of distribution.

Distribution is the bottleneck, but what is it that holds up distribution? Mainly one thing: dedication! We see examples of dedication in the young Mormon missionary, the incessantly active Jehovah's Witness, the zealous Communist youth. But there are other examples of dedication which should move us Christians even more. Think of David, for instance, or Daniel, Joshua, or Gideon. Indeed, a whole parade of dedicated individuals marches by us in Hebrews 11, and we see that the only thing that shook the world then and will shake the world now is an army of dedicated men and women whose faith in God is plain for all to see.

Oh, for Christians who will throw pride and ambition and fear to the winds; who will move out into the streets to be counted fools for Christ; who will stand in markets and theatres and on university campuses; who will ring doorbells all day long and rejoice at each door slammed in their faces! Oh, for individuals who will look at the tons of books and tracts piled up in our publishing houses and church basements and decide that something must be done about it!

Oh, for some thinking people who will reflect a bit about the large volumes they have accumulated in their personal libraries, compared to the two-page tracts they have given their lost neighbours! Oh, for an army of Christians who will lose the spiritual myopia of merely tucking their Bibles under their arms, and will joyfully move out with a briefcase full of Gospel books and magazines, Bibles and New Testaments which will serve both as a wedge to open a door to a conversation and also as a testimony to press home the message of the Gospel!

May God burden you as you read the rest of this book to move out in this greatly neglected area of literature evangelism and encourage others around you to do the same.

2

The Power of the Printed Page

'The pen is mightier than the sword!' How often we hear it, but how little we heed it. Few have fully comprehended the power of the printed page to mould the minds of men, to produce uprisings and revolutions, to ruin reputations, and even to sway an entire nation into carrying out such atrocities as the liquidation of six million Jews during World War II.

Those who know something of the history of the Communist Revolution in China say that it was the printed page, pouring from Red presses, that guaranteed the success of the revolution. Most of the dictators of history have utilised the power of printed propaganda. Lenin, the man who led the Russian revolution, once said, 'Every Communist must be actively engaged in the distribution of atheistic literature.' Fortunately, God's people and the forces for good in the world have also used the printed page. So the battle for the minds of people everywhere goes on.

It is not only political literature which is so influential in the moulding of minds. Literature used in advertising and publicity greatly affects the thinking of those who read it. The pornographic literature which is so widely distributed today also makes a deep impact on the minds of its readers, whether consciously or subconsciously. With the invasion of pornography, including child pornography on the Internet, the church is being faced with a whole new, more subtle aspect of spiritual warfare in which it needs to engage seriously.

If there is such potential in literature which comes from the mind of man, how much more power there is in that which springs from the very mind of God. The Bible says, 'For the word of God is living and active. Sharper than any double-edged sword, it penetrates even to dividing soul and spirit, joints and marrow; it judges the thoughts and attitudes of the heart' (Heb. 4:12).

Entire books have been filled with the testimonies of people whose quest for Jesus Christ was initiated and often fulfilled through reading a Gospel tract, a portion of the Scriptures, a Christian book. Bakht Singh, a man who has been mightily used by God to build the church in India, is one of these. As a young Sikh in northern India, he had a deep hatred for the Lord Jesus Christ and for the Christians that he knew. When he was 16, he was given a Bible by the Bible Society for successfully passing an examination in the mission school in which he studied; but to show his hatred for it, that same day he tore it to pieces. More than ten years later he was in Canada as a student of agricultural engineering, and again a friend gave him a copy of the New Testament. This time he began to read it. Captivated by its message, he read through the four Gospels and alone in a hotel room gave his life to the Lord Jesus Christ. His own written testimony and books have now been published in many of the languages of India, and thousands have been strengthened through them.

The impact of the ministry of many of the greatest Christian leaders has been increased through their use of literature. John Wesley is best known for his preaching, but he was also a powerful writer and in 1782 founded Britain's first tract society. Martin Luther, John Calvin and many others reached millions through the tracts which they printed, and early missionaries such as William Carey and Adoniram Judson found that the greatest effect of their ministry was through the tracts which they distributed. In our own day, the Billy Graham Evangelistic Association has made great use of literature. The books of Dr Graham have been translated into dozens of languages; their monthly magazine *Decision* is read by millions around the world; and the follow-up materials given to the thousands who decide for Christ at the Graham Crusades have helped many who have taken their first step in following Christ.

As we listen to the testimonies of those who have found Christ from many different backgrounds in all parts of the world, we discover that in the majority of cases literature played some part in their conversion. Perhaps it was only a Bible text printed on a poster that caught their eye, the message of a Gospel tract, or the written testimony of another whose life had been changed by Christ. The words that they read made an impact upon their minds and later bore fruit as they came to the Lord Jesus Christ.

We should never underestimate the power of other forms of evangelism, because it is not literature that is powerful, but the Gospel. Whether it is preached over the radio or television, from the pulpit of a church or on a street corner, or shared by a Christian with a friend, the Gospel is the 'power of God for salvation'. At the same time, however, the effectiveness of all other forms of evangelism can be greatly increased as literature is used with them. Some practical applications of this include:

1. A copy of an evangelistic message for those who were unable to attend the service.
2. Correspondence courses to follow up a radio or television broadcast.

3. A Gospel pamphlet given out after a street meeting or personal conversation.
4. A card giving one's web site, e-mail or mailing address so that there can be more contact.
5. A video, audio cassette or CD that presents the Word in some kind of message.

In this way different kinds of evangelism complement each other. As you develop the habit of passing on literature to those you meet and speak to about Christ, and as you look for other opportunities to use literature, you will find that its power will begin to make itself felt in the lives of those whom you contact.

3

The Power of a Consistent Life

The world has never seen such a demonstration of power as when God dressed Himself in human flesh. The power of the greatest atomic explosion devised by mankind today cannot begin to compare with the power manifested in the life of Christ. Indeed, what could be more powerful than God's eternal law lived out in perfection by Jesus Christ, the Word Incarnate? His life clarified the age-old law given to Moses and exemplified it for all generations to come. His was the power to create, to heal, to cast out demons, to control nature; and, greater than all these, the power to save and transform human lives.

The great motive which brought Him to earth, caused Him to weep with compassion over the multitudes and lay down His life for us, was love. God is love, and love is the most active and powerful force in existence to move the lives of individual human beings.

His teachings? They were impossible, contrary to all human nature. To many, they were only ideals or theories. Yet He lived them! Behind every word He uttered was the authority of a perfect life in absolute accord with all that He taught. So it is today. Those who advocate the teachings of Christ, whether in private testimony, public preaching or literature distribution, must have a life to back them up. The apostle Paul says to the Thessalonians, 'our gospel came to you not simply with words, but also with power, with the Holy Spirit and with deep conviction. You know how we lived among you for your sake' (1 Thess. 1:5). Paul's life as well as his speech was a presentation of the Gospel. This has been true of great Christians throughout the history of the church of Christ. The world is not interested in theory but in reality. One compassionate life of love will accomplish far more than a thousand well-prepared sermons or a ton of Christian literature.

If it seems strange to include this chapter in a book on literature evangelism, let us remember that the Word of God clearly teaches that God's instruments for world evangelism are His people: fearless, loving, Spirit-filled people who are moved by the love of God to do anything, anytime, anywhere, and at any cost, exactly as the Holy Spirit directs. Literature distribution, as every other form of the Lord's work, is greatly hindered by unreality in our lives. Our conduct, our speech, our appearance and our work are the things that the world notices more quickly than anything else. Unless our life is a life of compassion, even the literature we give out will be like a 'resounding gong or a clanging cymbal'. I believe we can paraphrase 1 Corinthians 13 to read, 'and though I give out Gospel tracts by the millions and have not love, I am nothing'. You may give out 5000 tracts a day. People may smile and say, 'How nice,' but if they see that your life is inconsistent with the message you distributed, they will inwardly scream at you: 'Practise what you preach!'

This does not mean that you have to be perfect to be a witness for Christ; nor does it mean that you must live under false pretences. It does mean that you must be in a right relationship to Jesus Christ and living in obedience to Him. If you are aware of some particular fault in your life, such as pride, jealousy, laziness, or selfishness, be honest to acknowledge it and trust Christ for victory over it. The people around you do not expect perfection, but they look for sincerity. They recognise and hate hypocrisy. If they see you progressing in some areas, winning victories which you attribute to the living Lord within you, they will respect you.

As you study this book, which in its remaining chapters is mainly of a practical nature, I

trust you will not forget that a power far
greater than that of the literature you give out
is the power of the life you live. In reality, it is
no longer your life but that of Jesus Christ
within you. The only thing more powerful than
the written Word of God is the Word incarnate
– Jesus Christ Himself living in broken and
empty vessels.

The following pages will mean little in the
long run if we do not become those vessels, and
do not present our lives as a living sacrifice to
God. This will be no easy road, but Christ never
promised that it would be. It will be a road of
self-denial, of forsaking all, of cross-bearing,
of following hard after Him. It will be a road to
death to self, for Calvary is the place of death.
Then the compassionate life of Jesus can move
through us with power, consuming all who
come in contact with it.

My prayer is that, as you continue to study
the practical aspects of effective literature evangelism, you will realise with the apostle Paul
that the Gospel is 'Christ in you, the hope of
glory', … which is the most powerful force on
earth!

4

Every Christian a Distributor

The Bible does not teach that pastors, missionaries, or other 'full-time' workers are to be God's sole instruments for evangelisation. On the contrary we see in Acts 8:4 that it was ordinary Christians, scattered because of persecution, who went everywhere preaching the Word.

Every believer is part of God's great plan and all work must be done for the glory of God. We must break down that wall between the secular and the sacred. The Bible teaches that every Christian is to be engaged in evangelism, bearing witness to the things which they have seen and heard. Not all are gifted preachers, but all of us have the ability to communicate with others. Christ's command to be a witness is a command to communicate to people everywhere the Gospel of Jesus Christ of which we have had personal experience and can speak with authority.

There is nothing new in this. Most Christians will read what I have written and agree whole-heartedly. Yet, more often than not, it is lip assent without leg action. For when it comes down to the actual work, very few are really willing to be witnesses. Many also don't seem to understand that their so-called secular work matters to God. There are no second-class citizens in God's Kingdom.

A small percentage of all churches conduct a systematic programme of visiting homes in their neighbourhood, and only a handful of their members participate in it. Unfortunately this visitation programme often consists of nothing more than invitations to attend church services, rather than presenting the claims of Christ and attempting to plant Christian literature in people's homes. This is a major lost opportunity, because literature can have a profound effect on people's ideas. For instance, after being arrested in the Soviet Union a number of years ago for distributing Christian literature, my interrogators confronted me with many of the arguments found in atheistic Communist literature. I saw that they firmly believed the arguments which they had read and which they now put to me. They granted me permission to visit the local bookstore in Rovno, where I bought at a very low price volumes of Marx and Lenin as well as various other books. They also gave me one book entitled *The Funny Bible*. The author had been trained in a Jesuit college in France. Having grown disillusioned with religion as he knew it, he had left the Roman Catholic Church, wanting to disclose the hypocrisy of the Jesuits, and had become a journalist in Paris. The preface of the book states: 'With a remarkable humour he tears to pieces the crudities and contradictions of the Bible, analysing its legends in detail.'

Since I first wrote *Literature Evangelism* we have seen the so-called collapse of Communism, although Communism is still alive in China and a few other places. However, the atheistic and humanistic teach-ing is as widespread as ever, having penetrated even the religious world more than we care to admit. We could write a whole book on the influence of liberal and unbelieving literature in our universities and theological colleges.

It is not my purpose to present a further challenge as to why every Christian should be a distributor. I wish rather to give some simple pointers as to how all Christians can be involved in literature evangelism, regardless of occupation, available spare time or special abilities. Below I have listed a few broad areas in which you will find the distribution of literature a spontaneous and convenient method of witnessing for your Lord.

1 At your place of employment

Unless your work demands that you travel a great deal, or you work alone, you probably work with basically the same group of individuals each day. Because of this your daily walk before your fellow workers will either lend weight to each piece of literature you give out or it will render it practically useless. Make sure the distribution of Christian literature on the job is a means of clinching your consistent testimony.

Since you ordinarily will have more than a casual contact with those with whom you work, it is generally better to approach them one by one rather than use the mass approach. A personal conversation, personal interest and privacy all help towards a more ready acceptance of the literature.

Right at the start, two cautions are in order. First, don't become known as a person who pushes tracts down everybody's throat! And secondly, don't use your employer's time to your own advantage. Don't be looking up Christian web sites during working hours, and don't bother someone when they are trying to work.

Now for some specific opportunities to distribute Christian literature:

a. *Take advantage of your lunch hours and breaks*.
   Have a variety of good tracts and booklets

with you at all times. Sometimes you can read a tract when someone else is around and then say casually, 'This leaflet's quite interesting about such-and-such an issue. Would you like to have a look?' Or, 'Have you ever seen this booklet? It's one of the most interesting stories I've read. If you'd like to read it, I'd be interested to know what you think of it.'

b. *Be alert to openings in the conversation.* Religion is often a topic of conversation. Many times your fellow workers will focus on a question or problem in which some of them have a genuine interest. This can be your opportunity. Knowing that you are a Christian, they may ask your opinion.

Don't pretend to know all the answers, but know where to find them. Have on hand Christian books relating to such subjects as science, archaeology and Bible criticism, as well as books which answer specific questions concerning salvation or the Christian life. Then, in the course of a conversation you might say, 'This book has some good ideas on this problem. Maybe you could find time to read it.'

c. *Keep handy a supply of cards offering a good course of home Bible studies or addresses for Christian web sites.* As your companions become more interested in spiritual things, offer them these cards and suggest that they

write for the course or check out the web site.
Perhaps several will be interested and you
can arrange to meet periodically with them
to study the lessons. This is ideal, because
then the ministry of literature evangelism
will be strengthened by your personal witness.

d. *Reach every fellow employee with the Word*.
Possibly the best means of doing this is
through the post. You must take a real interest in people. A Christmas or birthday card
perhaps with a good tract might be a way of
reaching some.

e. *Sell books whenever possible*. Bookselling on
the job may be difficult depending upon the
occupation and the amount of free time
employees enjoy. However, there are usually
no restrictions on lunch-hour activities.
Whenever possible, use these moments to
read a good book. Sooner or later someone
will ask you what you are reading. The door
is then open to recommend the book to your
friend.

When it becomes known that your 'hobby'
is selling books, opportunities will multiply.
You can keep a briefcase full of sample books
at your desk or in your locker. When someone says, 'My boy has a birthday next week',
or 'It's a real problem to know what to buy
for an invalid aunt', bring out your sample
case and show them a good selection of

books. If you make a note of what each of your colleagues buys, you can later follow through by asking if they have yet had an opportunity to read the book and how they liked it. You will also want to keep them in mind when new books come out by the same author, or related to the subject in which they are interested.

With prayer and patience and a consistent testimony, the interest may spread until permission could be granted to you to set up a permanent book table in some corner of the lounge or office. There employees could browse, and when they find a book which interests them they could see you. Various factors will influence the possibility of this, of course; and where it is possible, you will have the responsibility for keeping the display neat and attractive.

More practical than a permanent display in most cases would be a temporary one, perhaps during the period running up to Christmas or during National Book Week. Be alert to such special dates and take advantage of them. You may get permission to have a special meeting in which you could speak briefly on the importance of good literature, compared to the vast amount of pornographic and atheistic literature published today. Emphasise that the latter contributes to the demoralisation of a country, while good literature strengthens the character of a nation.

Keep in mind that in some cultures and situations this strategy is not possible. What I write in this book needs to be contextualised into your own culture and situation. Let's, however, be creative and look for other ways to get the Word out. Take advantage of contacts with other employees away from the job. Whenever possible visit their homes or invite them to your home. Some professions offer little opportunity for getting together away from the job, but many others, including nursing and military service, give unlimited opportunities to put good books and the Word of God into the hands of fellows workers.

It is a sound policy to emphasise that you are not selling to earn money, but as a representative of your church or Christian organisation. Make it clear that the profit goes solely towards the purchasing of more literature. We have also learned that in some situations giving or loaning a book, tape or video is more acceptable than trying to sell it. This is where we need to learn to raise money for such purposes. Over the years we learned the hard way how the lack of funds hinders what we are trying to do. OM now have a cassette tape, *Does the lack of funds hinder God's work?* and I hope you will listen to it.

2 Where you do your shopping

Some of the easiest places to give out Christian literature are the stores in which you do your shopping. No storeowner wants to lose a faithful customer, and if accepting and reading a small pamphlet will keep a customer, the owner will usually be happy to do so. Nor will an employee want to be reprimanded by their employer for refusing to accept a Christian pamphlet from a customer. People whose products you regularly buy will seldom object to buying something from you from time to time. They may understand your motive better if you mention that you are selling for your church or young people's group or in conjunction with a Christian literature campaign. Many who participate in our programme carry a small selection of books in their handbag or shopping bag. In a quiet moment when the proprietor has time to talk, out comes an appropriate book with a friendly word about it.

If you remember that you are not forcing something undesirable upon them but rather doing them the favour of offering them something they desperately need, you can be used effectively to reach your grocer, chemist, barber, banker, doctor, dentist and many others. Why not suggest that your doctor or dentist take out a subscription to a good Christian periodical, to leave in the waiting room for their patients to read? Of course, you need to remember that your ultimate goal is not to distribute tracts or to sell books, but to see men and women come to know Christ. The tract or book is only a means to an end, and will require much prayer and personal follow-up.

3 On the streets

How often we walk down the road in our own little world, completely oblivious to the people around us. Sometimes we are no more conscious of people for whom Christ died than we are of the telephone poles at the side of the road. As we begin prayerfully to give tracts to people we pass on the street, we will find that God will give us opportunities to stop and talk with some.

If you live in a small town, street distribution is neither practical nor necessary. In large cities where the population is great, you can distribute tracts daily with little likelihood of duplication. Is there an element of the population in your area which speaks a foreign language? Even if you cannot speak their language you have a wonderful opportunity to reach them with literature in their language. Memorise a few phrases in that language, and use them as you give them the literature. Anyone can learn a few sentences in another language, even in Chinese or Hindi. 'Here is a little booklet for you. It's free!' is all you need to say. Just watch the look of appreciation it brings to the face of the stranger in your country who doesn't speak your language.

4 In public places

Every trip that you take presents new opportunities for distribution. Buses, trains, boats and planes all provide opportunities to give Christian literature to your fellow passengers. Take books and tracts with you when you travel by car, and then leave them with petrol attendants, hitch-hikers, waitresses or policemen.

Couldn't our summer vacations count for eternity if Gospel seeds were sown in the places in which we stay? Restaurants, picnic areas, parks and beaches provide excellent opportunities for outreach. There is no better way to tour a country than by 'tracting' it.

5 In your own home

The best center of all for Christian witness is a Christian home. Here opportunities abound for those whose responsibilities are within the house. Every knock on the door provides opportunities to share our faith with friends, neighbours, traders, repairmen and many others. Many times unexpected interruptions provide opportunities which can be bought up for eternity!

What a wonderful thing it would be if every Christian family had Christian booklets available for visitors, as well as a few good books for sale. If you enter wholeheartedly into this ministry you will soon discover that your own home has become a powerful centre for evangelistic activity and literature outreach.

6 Through the post

There is almost no limit to the ways in which postal services can be utilised for spreading Gospel literature. Why not enclose a good tract the next time you pay your phone bill? Do the same with other bills, adding a short note of appreciation for their services. Sending follow-up literature by post to people with whom you have spoken during the day is a vital ministry which will be discussed more fully in Chapter 13.

Another excellent way to use the post is, for those who have the time, to collect names and addresses of people in foreign countries to whom you can send literature. This might be through pen-pal agencies or through personal friends, and often offers a good chance for personal correspondence as well as the opportunity to witness for Christ. Many also have their own web sites and use them to present the Gospel. We have heard of thousands coming to Christ through this method.

This chapter does not begin to exhaust the ways in which you can distribute Christian literature. In our daily lives we cross the paths of so many individuals that we cannot truthfully say we have no time to distribute literature. We can rationalise, we can bow to our own fears and negligence, we can surrender to shyness or unbelief, or we can go to God in prayer and ask Him for the boldness that comes when the Holy Spirit rules in a Christian's life. We read in Acts 4:31: 'After they prayed, the place where they were meeting was shaken. And they were all filled with the Holy Spirit and spoke the word of God boldly.' When this happens, you will see in your own life the sequel to this chapter, 'Every Christian a Distributor'.

5

Distribution of Free Christian Literature

Although distributing Gospel tracts may appear to be a simple thing, it can be a little difficult. It is one thing to give out a tract, but quite another to do so in such a way that the person receiving it will want to read it. Even though your contact with the person receiving the tract is extremely short, it can have a lasting effect for good or bad. Below are some practical points which will help you to be effective in tract distribution.

1 Be neatly dressed and attractive

How sad it is that some Christians allow themselves to become so unattractive in their appearance. There is no virtue in this. Paul became 'all things to all men' so that he might win some people for Christ. We must be neatly dressed if we want to reach a world that is interested only in things which are well presented.

People will judge us by our appearance, and their estimation of us will often determine whether or not they read the tract we offer them.

2 Be friendly and happy

A smile can often be an important factor in getting someone to accept or read a piece of Christian literature. It is hard to resist a smile, and a joyful appearance is an essential asset for effective literature distribution.

3 Be bold and at ease

People soon sense when someone is fearful and ill at ease. If, as you give out tracts, you show a ready-to-run attitude, people will class you as just another person who should be committed to a mental institution. We should give out literature as if we were passing out ten-pound notes to poor people. The Gospel is Good News; it is the power of God to salvation. So be bold and fearless.

4 Let the person receiving the tract feel that they are doing you a favour

Most people will never admit that they need help. But many are often willing to help others to some extent, especially if it does not take much effort. By saying, 'Thank you very much' as you give out a tract, you make it very hard for the person to refuse it. This is perhaps the best thing to say, particularly when a crowd is rushing past. Other useful sentences when presenting tracts are:

- 'Here is something for you to read when you get home. Thank you.'
- Here is something very important for you to read. Thank you.'
- 'Have you received one of these yet?' The answer will probably be 'No' or 'What is it?' Then hand over the tract, saying, 'It's a very important offer that you should know about.'
- 'Here is a free pamphlet for you. Thank you.'
- 'It's free!' This can be used when the crowd is coming quickly and you have no time to say more.

5 Take the literature to them

Don't expect people to come and ask you for the tracts. Go to them holding out the tract, as if you would be surprised if they did not take it. When people do refuse, one of these sentences may cause them to change their minds.

- 'It's free,'' or 'It doesn't cost anything.'
- 'Please take it. It will only take a minute to read.'
- 'You can take it. It doesn't weigh much!' If you can get a person to smile, they will usually accept your tract. Humour can break down the barrier of refusal.

Never force a tract on anyone. The words 'Well, thank you anyway' are sometimes appropriate when you meet with a definite refusal.

6 Be sure you are using good tracts

It is very important that the tracts we distribute should be well written and well printed. It is ideal if the tract is written by a national of the country in which it will be used, but in any case it should be adapted especially for that land. If at all possible, it should be printed within the country, so that it does not have anything foreign in it, such as 'Printed in the USA.'

Be certain that there are no typographical or grammatical errors in the tracts to be used. We need to be sure that they are doctrinally sound and at the same time that the wording is not so theological that the person in the street cannot understand it.

It is important to keep in mind that different kinds of tracts are good for different types of people. Therefore, it is wise to carry an assortment and to use them as you make personal contacts, trying to give each person the tract which best suits their need. For this reason I feel that the best way to distribute tracts is through personal contact. In this way you can come to understand the person's specific need and choose the tract accordingly.

When tracts are being selected for general distribution, they must be selected both for making contact and for planting a seed in the heart of the recipient. We have found in recent years that 'letter tracts' have produced the best results. These tracts, written in the form of a personal letter, usually present several reasons why the person should write in to receive more information concerning the Bible or the plan of salvation. A coupon on the tracts makes it convenient for the person reading it to send in their name and address requesting more free Gospel material. Usually the ones who respond are sent a correspondence course, which is one of the most effective means of carrying out literature evangelism.

Across the world the Jesus film and video has been one of the greatest evangelistic tools in the history of the church. We have found that using literature and especially New Testaments goes hand in hand with this kind of ministry. It is not either/or, but all kinds of ministry flowing together under the direction of the Holy Spirit.

Often, giving literature together with an invitation to a special event proves to be the link in the chain that brings someone to Christ. Sometimes literature given in conjunction with mime and music ministry leads to a real conversion to Christ.

7 Ready to go?

Where will you go? Some of the places you will want to consider are:

a. *Railway or bus stations* People found here will often be waiting for a while after receiving a tract, so there is a better chance of their reading it. The attendant in the station may eventually ask you to move on. If they do, accept the request graciously.
b. *House to house* In my opinion, in many countries this is the best type of distribution. I recommend taking time to speak with people as the Lord gives opportunities. It is good also to sell books when you are going from house to house, but at times when you want to distribute the maximum amount of literature in a limited time, you can simply place tracts in letter boxes.
c. *Market places* These are good places in many countries because of the large number of people who can be found there. Many will

put the tracts into their shopping bags to read when they get home.

d. *Street corners* For rapid distribution these are the best places, especially during the rush hour! When the crowd slows down, however, remember that you will contact more people if you go after them, rather than standing in one place and giving only to those who come straight toward you. It is very easy to get lazy after spending hours on the same corner, but this kind of laziness could mean that people will be eternally lost! If someone is lost, and we know that Christ loves them and has died for them, we should certainly want to go out of our way to reach them.

e. *Buses, trains, etc.* These are ideal places to distribute tracts. With a friendly smile you can go from one end of the train to the other, giving everyone something to read along the way. It will take boldness, but unless God gives us holy boldness we will never reach the world with the Gospel.

f. *Hospitals, prisons and other institutions* In these places you will need to obtain permission. If it is given, you will have a great opportunity.

g. *Universities, schools and large offices* These are good places to go at a time when people are coming out. Young people are often more ready to receive literature than adults. On the other hand, they may laugh at you. At such times, look to the Lord and ask Him for grace.

h. *Through the post* Letter-tracts are ideal for sending through the post, and they usually yield a higher result when used in this way. There are any number of places from which addresses can be obtained. You can start with the telephone directory and the newspaper.

8 Wherever you go!

This is really the key to distributing God's word. Just imagine what would happen if Christians spontaneously gave out literature wherever they went. Tract distribution should be a part of us, not just something to do when we are on a special campaign, or with a team, but something we are doing all the time, wherever we happen to be.

Much more could be said concerning the ministry of literature distribution, but more than anything else, we need to get started in actually doing it. Experience is the best teacher: you can read books on the subject, but that will never take the place of getting out on the job.

Thousands of people have been converted as a result of books, tracts and correspondence courses. Millions could be reached in this way. The bottleneck is you! Unless you are willing to go at it and stick at it, the millions will never be reached. It is one thing to give out tracts once a week or once a year. It is quite another thing to be using your free time constantly to give out literature and present Christ to those who need Him, keeping in mind the importance of each individual you meet and always being ready to follow up any who show interest.

In OM over the past 40 or more years, we have distributed literature, cassettes and videos to over one billion people.

6

Selling Christian Literature

Most people who have attempted to sell Christian books have come to realise that it is not easy. Many have begun, only to end up discouraged, defeated, and without any desire to continue in this ministry.

Sometimes the reason has been that they have not depended on the Lord to move in the hearts of people. There can be no substitute for the work of the Holy Spirit of God. But over the years we also discovered in many Christians a lack of grace and sensitivity in the way they deal with people, a tendency to be judgmental and legalistic. So many believers find it hard to even have a conversation with someone, much less try to sell them a book. Charles Swindoll's book *The Grace Awakening* and similar material has been greatly used to change our lives. That is why in my new book *Out of the Comfort Zone* I have given such a strong plea to bring more grace into everything we do.

In this chapter I hope to give a few simple instructions on how to sell Christian books that will enable you to move forward with success in this very important ministry.

One of the main reasons for the lack of distribution of Christian books today is that very few men and women have been trained in the art of selling Christian literature. Some people think that all literature should be given freely without charge. However, most Christians agree that it is better to sell books and magazines, while freely distributing tracts and small booklets. Charges should be made for certain types of Christian literature for the following reasons:

1. In most countries there is a feeling that only propaganda is free, and propaganda is by definition unwanted.
2. People generally appreciate the things that have cost them something. It is unlikely that they will buy a book they do not intend to read. This means that your literature will be distributed to those who are really interested in reading it.
3. Selling literature avoids suspicion, which is often aroused when something is offered free.
4. Selling literature enables some people to go into Christian literature distribution full time, using the profits from the sale of

literature to support themselves and their families.

5. One of the primary purposes of having a Christian bookstore is to sell books and other related materials that can show God's love and be a help in people coming to know Christ. It can be a real Gospel centre for sending out Christian literature and for winning lost souls to Jesus Christ. In most shops the profit from the sale of books can be used to cover the rent and pay the salaries of the workers.

6. Selling Christian literature can help make the work in various countries indigenous from the beginning. This is undoubtedly a very important factor in evangelism and the eventual establishment of new churches.

7. Selling subscriptions to Christian magazines opens doors for a systematic presentation of the Gospel each month as these magazines enter homes.

8. The sale of books makes it possible for some Christian publishers and workers to get Christian literature on the secular news-stands and in secular bookstores.

9. In the long run more literature can be distributed by selling than by giving away since the profits from the sale of books can be used to publish more books. This is known as the revolving-fund plan.

Having seen the reasons for selling Christian books, we must next learn how to sell them. One of the first things we must have is a teachable spirit. One who is not willing to learn will never be successful in selling books, and the greatest traders in the world never stop learning about salesmanship.

In any kind of selling there are certain vitally important things that you must know:

a. *Your product*

You must not only be familiar with the books you are selling, but you must also be enthusiastic about them. Remember, enthusiasm sells!

b. *Your prospect*

It is important to know people, their needs, and their way of thinking. Each person with whom you speak is different, and you need to become conscious of the fact that people are individuals with personal needs. Your responsibility as a Christian bookseller is to provide them with literature that will point them to the Christ who can meet every need.

c. *How to arouse interest*

The bookseller must somehow arouse the interest of the prospective buyer. My belief is that the greatest interest is aroused by the Holy Spirit moving in answer to prayer. At the same time, the various approaches presented in detail in Chapters 10–12 help to accomplish this important objective. Be sure to study them, and memorise as many as possible. They could be one of the key factors in enabling you to become a successful distributor of Christian books.

d. *How to speak*

Some retailers have said that the most important thing in selling is to know what to say, when to say it, and how to say it! Reading books on public speaking and on salesmanship can be a tremendous help. Although they will have many ideas which are of little value for the Christian, I highly recommend that anyone doing Christian literature distribution read books on these subjects. Salesmanship is not something which is learned overnight. It takes years of study and experience before most salespeople develop real selling ability. However, the best way to learn is by doing! Begin right now to talk to people about Jesus Christ and to present people with Christian books.

When someone buys a book from you, ask yourself, 'What was it that captured their interest? What caused them to buy this book?' If you develop the practice of learning why people buy particular books, you will soon learn the approaches demanded for specific occasions. Personal preparation is an important part of this phase of knowledge. The person who goes out to distribute Christian books either spiritually or practically unprepared will end up sooner or later very discouraged and without many results.

Again, it is important to remember that our main task is never that of selling books, but always that of being ambassadors for Christ and making Him known. As we go to the door of a home we should go prayerfully, trusting that God will open the way not only to sell or distribute some Christian literature, but also to give a word of testimony for the Lord Jesus and if at all possible to lead that soul to the Saviour. We must never allow worldly aims to creep into our work. Our goal is not to earn money; it is not to enter into competition to see how many books we can sell; nor is it to prove that we are good at selling. Our task is to present the love of God, expressed through the atoning death of Christ Jesus, to lost men and women so that they can turn to Him and find life!

For this reason, rather than going out to sell books, many Christians prefer to go out to witness for Jesus Christ and to give books to interested people in exchange for a donation. This may seem very similar to selling, but the two methods are actually quite distinct. In the one case a definite price is asked for the book; in the other the book is given in exchange for a donation which could be more or less than the actual value of the book. The method of receiving donations is especially effective in countries where it is difficult to obtain a colportage or salesman's licence.

The greatest temptation in the work of selling Christian literature is discouragement. There will be days when you may sell very few books, and if your goal, even subconsciously, is to 'sell', on those days you will be very discouraged, thinking your time has been wasted. Even when you cannot sell a Scripture portion, a Gospel book or magazine, if you leave free literature in each home, then your time will not have been wasted.

In Galatians 6:9 we read that we should not 'become weary in doing good, for at the proper time we will reap a harvest if we do not give up'. You cannot trust your feelings in this type of work, for you will probably find that you almost never 'feel' like selling or visiting from house to house. You must remember that God has not commanded us to move out and evangelise according to our feelings, but rather He has told us to go forth by faith. In Christian bookselling we must not fix our eyes on the sales, but rather keep them on the Saviour and what He will do in the hearts of the people we contact, if we will only believe Him for great and mighty things!

This chapter has focused on selling books in homes, shops and on the street. When I first wrote this book I was only just discovering the

importance of having a church book table and
selling books at meetings. Over the years, however, this has proved to be one of the most
effective ways to get the Word out, and I want
to underline here the importance of this addi-
tional opportunity to sell Christian literature.
We are speaking here of books going into the
hands of millions of people!

7

House-to-House Distribution

Literature evangelism house-to-house holds many exciting opportunities for people who will deliberately seek them out, although in some countries, such as India, going shop-to-shop and office-to-office has proved easier and more effective. We want to consider some of these opportunities in this chapter. First, however, some preparatory steps.

1.1 Prayer

The first and most important preparation is prayer. Unless your work is saturated with prayer, all the suggestions I can give will become mere gimmicks which at best can only serve to accomplish a commercial 'selling' job. What good are books that are sold if they are not read and if the Spirit of God does not reveal the truths in them?

1.2 Literature and other materials

These should be carefully selected according to the economic level of the area in which you plan to distribute. For instance, if you are going to a new housing area where many young married couples live, you will want to take a good supply of books for children. Using children's books, tapes or videos is a great way to open doors. If you are considering a poor area, it is a good idea to stock up on magazines and Gospels of John. In settled residential areas where many professional people live you will need high-quality books, both in form and content. You should also be aware of the worldwide campaign using the *Jesus* video, in which the whole church is mobilized. Sometimes Christians sell it; other times they loan it out or give it for a donation. It is exciting strategy that is bearing much fruit.

Literature should be packed neatly into a briefcase or carrying bag which need not be expensive, but should be strong and durable. It is important to protect the literature carefully to avoid getting it soiled. Dirty, dog-eared books or magazines make a poor impression on those you wish to win.

1.3 Materials

If you plan to devote an entire day or longer to literature distribution, the following list of suggested materials might be of help. These are not essential, but during literature campaigns we have discovered that they often help to make the work run more smoothly and effectively.

a. *A map of the area in which you will be working* If you are doing systematic house-to-house visiting, this is important when it comes to marking off the streets, block by block.

b. *A pen and a small notebook* These are for jotting down names and addresses of interested individuals or other notes you want to remember.

c. *Money* If you plan to be selling books, you should have enough loose change in an easily accessible but secure place.

d. *A plastic bag or a sheet of plastic* This can be used to protect the books should you be caught out in the rain.

e. *A pair of comfortable walking shoes* This is more important than you may think. Continual walking on hard pavements or country roads, up and down stairs, carrying heavy book bags, is never easy work and becomes almost unbearable if your feet are hurting.

One last suggestion before we move into specific areas of distribution. If you are working with a group, before dispersing for distribution see that watches are synchronised and each person knows exactly where to meet again and at what time.

One of the greatest advantages of house-to-house visiting is that it is systematic – a sure means of reaching an entire community or city if you plan to be there for an extended period. Here you will meet people in their own environment, in a relaxed, informal, often hospitable atmosphere. It is in their own homes that people feel free to be themselves, and thus it is that many times it is in the privacy of the home that God can most clearly speak to individuals, either through a verbal testimony or through a piece of Gospel literature – or both.

Specific approaches, which should be carefully studied until they are mastered, will be presented in chapter 10. However, it is my purpose here to give some practical advice: most of it is common sense, but nevertheless there are details we need to be reminded about.

2.1 As you approach the door

Be organised! It is good to have a few books in your hands ready for an immediate smooth presentation as soon as the door opens. Take note of your surroundings. Notice any detail which may be helpful in your contact with the occupants, such as toys in the yard which let you know there are children; milk outside the door which may mean the family is not at home; a name-card or plaque, the sign of a profession, or some other clue as to what kind of family you are visiting.

If the door to a block of flats is locked, you should ring either the caretaker or one of the first-floor apartments. You will occasionally find buildings or areas where selling is prohibited. Technically and legally you are not 'selling' books when you offer them for unspecified donations. If you are questioned on this point either by a police official, a caretaker or a private citizen, explain exactly what you are doing and why, and you will often be permitted to continue. If you are still asked to leave then do it graciously, leaving free literature with the individual.

As you approach a building you will want to analyse it, noting the number of floors, doorways, mail boxes, etc., to determine more or less the number of families who live there. This work calls for an adventurous spirit. In order not to bypass families who are in need of the Word, you will have to investigate, ask questions, and search earnestly.

Be prepared for anything! This is the wonderful, exciting part of visitation: you never know what lies behind the door, but you can be sure that you will have some of the most interesting experiences of your life visiting house-to-house.

2.2 While you are at the door

The habit of putting yourself in the place of the
other person will stand you in good stead in
this work. Remember that you are not expected
at this door, and your appearance will be a
surprise, especially if you are foreign to the
country in which you are visiting. Try not to
startle people by stepping suddenly toward
them when the door is opened or by approach-
ing them softly if they happen not to be looking
at you. If it is dark or there are shadows, stand
where the light will shine on you when the
door is opened and in a friendly voice quickly
explain your mission. When you work on the
sunny side of the street you can be sure of a
more ready acceptance if you stand in such
a way that you shade the face of the one who
answers the door. No one likes to get the bright
glare of the sun in their eyes.

As you speak with an individual at their
door, focus your attention on them. Avoid let-
ting your eyes stray curiously inside the house
or to other objects close at hand, but speak
directly to the person in an open, friendly manner. When presenting the books, hold them
towards the person so that the titles can be read
easily. Have books at your fingertips so you do
not have to fumble for them and bend down to
search through your bag, for this will inevitably
lose the attention of the person you are visiting.

If a child comes to the door and tells you they are alone at home, do not press the selling point. It is possible that the child's parents have left instructions not to open the door while they are absent, so do not frighten the child by persistence if they do not open it. Instead, slip a children's tract under the door along with tracts for parents.

You will sometimes be invited inside a home to continue a conversation or to show your books. This usually gives you a chance to spread out your books inside the house, and may afford an excellent opportunity for witnessing. Remember, however, that it is sometimes easy to confuse opportunities to witness with opportunities to converse. The latter will be many, especially if you are foreign to the country as people will naturally be curious about you. Some incidental conversation is good, but it can be very time-consuming and sometimes rather pointless. Your real purpose it to give testimony to the Lord Jesus, and if, after a few minutes of talk, there seems to be no opening to speak of spiritual things it is usually best to leave some free literature and excuse yourself, praying that the Lord will speak to them through this literature. Be careful not to do this abruptly, however, as you may offend the individuals who have offered you the hospitality of their home.

If, during the conversation, some spiritual interest is evident, endeavour to get the correct name and address. To avoid arousing suspicion or hostility, it is usually advisable to jot this down after leaving the home unless you explain your reason for doing it. You can say, 'Would it be possible for me to have your name and address so that I could correspond with you or send some literature that I don't have with me at the moment?' Then be sure to do it. Do not make the mistake of thinking that you will remember a name or address. It may be clear at the time but after a few more houses it will be forgotten unless you record it.

A word of caution in connection with entering homes: if a girl happens to be visiting alone and a man who is apparently alone in the house invites her to enter, she should normally decline. Similarly, it can sometimes be injurious to the reputation of a young man to enter at the invitation of a woman who is alone.

Since, in house-to-house work, you are entering private property, it is especially important that you do so with consideration and courtesy. Such seemingly small details as closing doors or wiping your feet before entering a home do much to leave a good impression. Indeed, your contact will usually be so brief that it is just such small details as these which will be remembered after you have left.

8

Distribution in Metropolitan Areas

The growth of cities and urban areas is a great phenomenon in our day. Opportunities for literature distribution abound in these areas where there are constant influxes of new people. If you plan to reach every home in a city you should join hands either with a church's young people's group, the entire church, or even a number of churches in the city. The opportunities to sell Christian books are almost unlimited in many cities, and if you have the opportunity it is always better to leave good books and portions of the Bible rather than only tracts. In the next few pages we want to look at some of the ways to take advantage of these opportunities to sell books. We know that false cults use some of these methods also, but that should not necessarily intimidate us. The secular world still uses some of these 'old-fashioned' methods to get their message out. Often, effective work is the right blending of the old and the new.

1 Book tables

As street vendors have discovered, strategic-
ally placed tables or booths are a good means
of attracting the attention of passers-by.
Shoppers, individuals out for an afternoon
walk, students or businessmen during their
lunch-hour are all potential customers who
occasionally have spare moments to stop and
browse. So why not a table of Christian books?

This may be a collapsible table which can be
put up at a moment's notice, or it may be nothing more than a plank supported by two
carpenter's trestles and covered by paper or a
piece of cloth. It need not be anything fancy or
expensive. We often make the mistake of thinking that before attempting anything for the
Lord we must have the very best of equipment
when what is really important is that we begin.
A book display might even emerge sponta-
neouly when passers-by indicate an interest in
the books you have to sell. This has happened
more than once on our campaigns when books
were selling so well that the young people
arranged their literature in a window-ledge
display or on the bonnet of their car. A few
interested individuals soon attracted others
until a small group gathered around to look at
and purchase the books.

It might be mentioned here that one quality
which is essential for the Christian bookseller is

boldness – the boldness which comes from the Spirit of God and transcends all human personality traits. There is no room for self-consciousness when you are out on a street selling books for you will be looked at, laughed at, scoffed at and ridiculed. Again you must be prepared for anything. You can never fully anticipate what God has planned for you unless you take one step in His direction. Many times He does not open more opportunities until you have acted on the present one. The first step is always the hardest.

I remember an incident which occurred in Madrid one day when a small student group took a load of Roman Catholic Scripture portions to the flea market, not knowing exactly what they were going to do but praying that God would give them opportunities for distributing them. After scouting around they discovered that by paying a small fee they could have permission to set up a vendor's stand if they could find an empty space. Since they had no stand or materials for making one, they found a corner where many people passed and spread their books out in an attractive display on the pavement. Then they waited.

Nothing happened. A few people smiled as they passed by, but most merely stepped around the display. Finally, the young people decided that it was time to put aside all inhibitions or nothing would ever happen. So, with a prayer in their hearts, they picked up a handful of New Testaments and began to shout, 'Read the New Testament; the second part of the sacred Scriptures. Get the Epistles of St Paul here . . . only 16 pesetas.' The vendors on either side were highly amused and so were many passers-by, but others began to stop and listen; then they looked at the books and started to buy them. After this, the young people were so busy selling books that they had no time or need to attract attention by shouting. In three hours they sold many Bibles, New Testaments, and other portions of the Scriptures! There was no breakthrough until there was a willingness to be counted 'fools for Christ'.

A not-so-noisy, yet effective, means of calling the attention of people to your stand is to make attractive, eye-catching signs advertising one book, or perhaps offering it at a special price, and arranging the books on your table colourfully and attractively. Having a book display in conjunction with music or a drama presentation is a real winner in some places. Plan to push one book, and take a quantity of that title to pile conspicuously on the table. The titles of books are very important in themselves: one never knows the thoughts a title such as *World Aflame* might provoke in an individual passing by a book display.

Be sure to have a good range of music, audio and video cassettes, as well as follow-up material to get people to web sites or, better yet, a local church. It is usually necessary to obtain permission for setting up a book table either from local authorities or from the proprietors or managers of the particular location. This is usually granted readily if they are approached courteously.

The following are some of the most effective locations for setting up a display of literature:

- Shopping districts
- Market places
- Cinemas
- Tourist sites
- Squares or parks
- Fairs
- Sports grounds
- Carnivals
- Circuses
- Political meetings
- Parades
- University campuses

The use of book tables inside churches or at church conventions, camps and seminars merits special consideration. Permission should be secured well in advance from the pastor or those in charge of the occasion, and they should also be allowed to examine the books you are selling if they want to do so.

When you plan to sell to a predominantly Christian group you should select books and materials accordingly. Devotional, biographical and Bible-study books are all good. I have noticed, however, that often when Christians gather in these meetings it is to be saturated anew with spiritual truths which edify them, but which many times never result in a practical outworking through their lives. It is a good idea therefore to have on hand a good supply of evangelistic material produced especially for the unconverted, as it encourages Christians to buy books to sell to their friends and neighbours. The selection of books at such a table should not be limited to books solely for Christian people, but should include a number of books for the unconverted.

2 Bookmobiles

In many respects what applies to book tables also applies to the use of bookmobiles. These, like book tables, are not limited to cities but can be used wherever a crowd can be gathered. A bookmobile is usually a van containing shelves specifically for carrying books and with window space for displays. Some people have improvised satisfactory 'travelling bookstores' by using the tailboard of vans and estate cars, and some have used a caravan which has been converted into a mobile book unit. No matter what is used, the two important things to remember are: first, to display the books attractively; and second, to make certain the stock is securely packed so that jolting and rolling will not destroy the literature as the vehicle travels from place to place.

If you have access to a public-address system you can use this for giving book reviews or proclaiming the Gospel. A battery-operated cassette recorder or CD player is also a help in attracting attention, for most people respond favourably to good music.

Perhaps you have nothing which would be suitable for a bookmobile, but you do have a car. A Christian in Paris has very effectively used a tract rack which he carries in his car. Each time he has errands he parks in a conspicuous place, hooks the rack over the window, fills it with attractive pamphlets, and leaves. Passers-by see the sign inviting them to take one and help themselves to a tract. It has cost him very little time or effort yet it has enabled him to proclaim the Gospel.

3 Person-to-person

I have found this one of the most effective methods of distributing Christian literature and of opening the way to a conversation about Christ. This can be accomplished in such a wide variety of places that it is almost superfluous to mention them here. However, the following have been tried and found to be good distribution points in various countries.

- Railway stations
- Bus stations
- Universities
- Bars

- Airports
- Hotel lobbies
- Hospitals
- Pavement cafés
- Beaches
- Zoos

In each of these areas it is just a matter of selecting an individual who does not appear to be either hurried or very occupied, sitting down beside him and beginning a conversation. After exchanging greetings, you could say something like:

'I wonder if you have read this amazing new book?' (handing them one of your books).

'Are you familiar with this new magazine?'

'May I ask you what your opinion is of the New Testament?' (handing them a copy of the New Testament).

You must trust the Lord to guide in further conversation, because you can never anticipate the response of an individual. Don't be discouraged if many are terse or impolite, but look to the Lord to guide you to those with whom He would have you speak.

4 A newspaper-boy style

If you are in a crowd of people and have no type of book table, you might find it effective to sell books newspaper-boy style, possibly carrying a display sign with a cover of the book pasted on it, and shouting as you hold up the sign or even the books themselves. This method requires particular boldness and confidence and is better not even attempted than done with a tremulous, uncertain voice which will carry no weight whatsoever in a crowd of people. I vividly recall standing on the pavements of Chicago with the book *Science Speaks*, shouting loudly, 'New book proves the Bible to be the Word of God . . . get your copy today.' A good number of copies were sold in this way.

In each of the above-mentioned methods the important thing is to get started. Don't wait for it to become easy. It never will. It's hard work, and the only way to do it is to 'take up your cross and follow Him'. He, and He alone, can give you the motivation and strength to do it.

9

Distribution in Towns and Villages

Distribution of literature in small towns and rural areas differs in many ways from distribution in metropolitan areas. For one thing, you will not need to take any measures to attract attention. Your very presence will attract the attention of the community. For this reason you should be even more careful about your behaviour. In many countries, since the atmosphere in these areas is generally rather quiet and seldom interrupted by the out-of-the-ordinary, you can be certain that your visit will make an impression. You will want to do all you can to make that impression a good one. Even after your group has left, you will be discussed over the dinner table and in bars and barber shops, until a picture of you is formed by the whole community. The sudden appearance of a group of strangers in a small town cannot fail to arouse curiosity and sometimes even suspicion. 'What are they doing here?' will be whispered over back fences until the question is answered by personal contacts with some of the group. Every move will be watched from the moment of your arrival and even the make and location of your vehicle will be common knowledge.

By observing a few rules of conduct which apply especially to small towns you can reduce the barriers that sometimes exist between villagers and visitors from outside.

1. As you arrive, avoid confusion and disorganisation. Don't jump out of the car and begin making preparations with much talk and laughter. Above all, don't begin pointing out streets and directions for each to take. Do this inside the car and have bags ready so that you can leave as inconspicuously as possible. In some places it is good to check with the police and tell them what you are doing. Remember, they also need the Lord.

2. Be friendly and natural. It is surprising how the simplest things can break the ice. The world of most village people is small and the common things of life are of great importance to them. A genuine interest in such things as flowers, children, animals and music all tend to reduce the distance between you. While they resent 'foreign airs' they will respond to genuine friendliness.

3. Be interested but avoid being too inquisitive. Don't gaze around as if you find the people and their way of life rather quaint and amusing. It is good to admire sincerely their handiwork, but be careful not to remark indiscreetly about articles in their houses for this will often be mistaken as a hint that you would like to have them. In some countries, if people think they detect such an attitude, it is a custom to give you the admired article even though they may have no desire to part with it.

4. Be frank. There is a natural curiosity on the part of the people to know who you are, where you come from, and what you are doing. While you want to avoid engaging in long conversations with different individuals who will all ask basically the same questions, do take time to briefly respond to their questions. It is often better to answer them before they are even asked by saying something like, 'I am a student here with a group of young people to distribute Christian literature.' You can then proceed with your work as their minds will not be crowded with questions to ask the moment they have a chance. Often they will want to know about your country, commenting on such things as the economic or material advantages, or the employment situation. In most cases it is better to avoid such

conversations with a remark such as, 'I like your country very much and am finding the people very kind and friendly.' Remember that you are not there to discuss politics and economics but rather to tell them of God's great love for them.

5. Respect personal property. Don't litter the streets of their village with rubbish, or leave their gates hanging open behind you so the dogs and chickens can wander out. Be careful not to step on their flowers or the crops in a farmer's field.

6. As far as possible avoid speaking a foreign language in their presence. When people cannot understand what you are saying, they may feel that you are talking about them.

7. If you are working with a group, avoid laughing among yourselves. The towns-people could easily misunderstand and think that you are laughing at them.

8. At the same time be willing to laugh at yourself. There is probably no quality which will endear you so much to small-town people as the ability to laugh at yourself, especially if you make an obvious mistake.

9. Be humble. Avoid any trace of pride or snobbishness. There is nothing which will so estrange you from people as a sense of pride. Be careful not to disdain them either by look or action.

10. If you are in a store, wait your turn patiently. Don't finger their products as if you think they are inferior. Be friendly toward the shopkeeper, not suspicious or cold.

11. *Give special attention to conduct between men and women*. Your lives will be watched, and you should 'avoid all appearance of evil'. If you are in a mixed group, especially in small towns, it is better that women work with women and men with men. When the group is all together there should be no foolishness that could be misinterpreted.

With these things in mind, we can look at the principles of distribution in small villages. There will, of course, rarely be large crowds of people or the constant flow that is in a city. The best way to reach villages is by going from door to door. Here you may encounter people who will say truthfully that they have no money. Then you might mention that you will exchange books for produce such as fruit, eggs, or garden products.

There are a number of strategic spots to reach people in villages:

a. *In the park*

During the afternoon on fine days you will often find many children gathered here with their mothers. These women may be in little groups talking together as they watch the children. This provides a wonderful opportunity for you to approach them in a friendly manner and introduce yourself and your literature. When several women are together, one tends to do what the others do and if one agrees to buy a book, the rest will probably follow.

b. *At public wells or fountains*

This is another place at which women of the village often congregate, and while they will seldom have money with them there, if they are interested in a book they may return home and then send a child back with the money.

c. *At the door of the cinema*

During the evenings you will find many people gathered at the local cinema, where you can reach them as they stand in line or as they leave the building.

d. *In the market*

This is probably the best method to reach the majority of the village population in the shortest possible time. In some villages markets are held each day, but in most they are once a week. This is by far the busiest day of the week. You will do well to know the market days of different villages in advance and make it a point to be there. This is an ideal opportunity for book distribution, as from early morning the villagers will throng the market-place. They will have money with them and will already be disposed to buy. If you can park your bookmobile there or set up a table, or just fill your arms with books and start through the crowd, you are almost certain to have results.

e. *At factories or construction projects*

These are good places to reach the men of the village, especially during their lunch-hour or at closing time. It is sometimes possible to receive permission from the supervisor of a factory to speak with all the employees even during work hours.

f. *At barber's shops and bars*

These are also popular spots where men gather to chat when they have free time. They are usually open and interested in discussing new ideas and you will probably find a welcome in their midst.

g. *Banks, offices and stores*

There is far more likelihood of your gaining entrance in small-town businesses than in those of large cities because they are more loosely knit in their organisation. It is usually best to ask for the manager and then explain what your purpose is and ask for permission to speak with the staff. Often they will gather round as you are talking and you can take advantage of counter space to spread out a little display offering books to each of them to flick through as you talk. In this way you will frequently encounter individuals with keen spiritual interest who will take the time to select their books carefully. Of course, if you see that it is a busy period it is better to go and return later.

h. *Schools*

In many villages the schools are quite small, and it is sometimes possible to receive permission from the headteacher to address the students or to set up a small book exhibition in the school. You will want to have a sufficient quantity of Gospels or small Gospel booklets and tracts, so that each student will be able to receive a piece of literature if they wish.

i. *Holidays or fairs*

These are important days observed with special enthusiasm in most small towns, and you will usually find a prevailing festive mood which makes the people open to you. This is a good opportunity to reach people from outlying farms who are usually not part of the local community.

In some places people who live in small towns or villages have had far fewer opportunities to hear the Gospel than those in large cities. Therefore, in the short time you are there, you must make the most of your time by using every opportunity, praying that God will make these contacts count for eternity.

Printed material as well as television, video, CDs, cassettes and the Internet all effect what people believe and practice. So, let's continue to mobilise and flood the world with God's message in all of its many forms. We have also seen an explosion of holistic ministry. As God's people we are concerned about every aspect of a person's life and also the environment. Many books are now written about this, which is only one more proof of the power of the printed page. So let's continue to mobilize and flood the world with God's message in all its many forms.

10

Approaches

All too often the evangelical church has challenged young people and adults alike to the task of evangelism without teaching them how to go about it. Zeal without knowledge is frustrating, to say the least, and can be disastrous.

The purpose of this chapter is to show you exactly how you can make an effective approach in literature distribution. The following are tried and tested approaches which could prove to be of great value. Many of them are so general that they can be used by almost anyone. Others are basic ideas which you can adapt to your own situation. They should be studied and learned so thoroughly that you can use them freely and convincingly as a witness for the Lord. It is recommended that you choose several of these approaches, adapt them to your own needs, and memorise them. This will give you the confidence of knowing what to say when the door opens!

1 Student approach

In my opinion this is one of the best approaches and has been used successfully in many countries. It can be used effectively by young people, and differentiates them from the general flow of sales-people who are often unwelcome at the door. You are an individual studying for something so you have a purpose in life other than knocking on doors to sell books. This approach gives you personally a position. A favourable impression is strengthened when you say that you are with a group of young people. This erases the concept that you are an eccentric individual out alone in this house-to-house routine, and replaces it with the idea that this must be an important crusade if so many people are participating in it. Listed below are several variations of the 'student approach' which may be of help to you.

'Good morning. We are here with a group of international students who are using our holidays to distribute good literature . . .'

'How are you, sir? I am a student passing through your city with a group of young people. In order to learn your language a little, we are visiting different homes. At the same time as you help us by talking to us, we want to help you by offering a selection of good books which are important for everyone . . .'

In this approach, you will notice that we did not say 'We are students of "the" language", but rather, 'We are students of "your" language.' This may seem like an insignificant detail, but many times it accomplishes something very important: it makes the individual with whom you are speaking feel important, as you think their language is important enough to learn it and you want help from them.

'Good afternoon, I am a university student and am very interested in philosophy. While travelling through your country, I have been speaking to people about their philosophy of life. I have found that many people are searching for truth: they are looking for something that they can commit their lives to. I was also searching for that until I found what I was looking for in the Lord Jesus Christ, who said, "I am the Truth." He has changed my life, and I have some books with me which explain more thoroughly the message of Jesus Christ.'

2 Good literature approach

This is another 'non-religious' approach which gives you the authority of working with a group. It can be used with almost any type of person and the individual's response to this general introduction should give you a clue as to how to proceed from there.

'Good morning, Madam. We are with a crusade for good literature and we have a selection of good books for the whole family . . .' (This is the simplest and one which you can use if the person is obviously in a hurry.)

'Good afternoon. I am taking part in a literature crusade with an international group of young people who feel that every family should have the privilege of owning good books. I have here a selection which I am sure will be of interest to you . . .'

'How do you do? I am sure that you would agree with me that young people should be reading good books. We feel that this is very important and we are giving our holiday time to distributing some very good books for young people as well as for adults.'

3 Personal testimony approach

This is a good method when you immediately see that you have the attention of the person. The examples given show how this approach can be used, although you will need to adapt them to your own situation. Preparation is especially important, and you need to go out with a well-prepared presentation of your testimony linked with literature distribution.

'Good morning, sir. Could I have just a few minutes to speak with you about something that I
believe will be of interest to you? Perhaps you are
wondering if I am a salesman? Actually I am an
engineer. Not long ago I met someone who
changed my life completely, and during my holidays I am taking this opportunity to distribute
books which speak about Him: Jesus Christ. He is
the one who said, "I am come that they might
have life and have it more abundantly."'

'Good morning, madam. I know that you are
very busy this morning, but I believe that what I
have to say is very important. Only three years
ago I was a very confused young person. I had a
good job, many friends and all the money I
needed, yet my life seemed very empty. It was
through the message of the Bible that God
brought love and joy into my life. I've come this
morning to encourage you to read your Bible
more this week, because I know that it can add
much to your life. I also have some books with
me which present the message of the Bible.'

'Good afternoon, madam. I know that you are
very busy with your work in the house, because I
also work at home. I know that many mothers
sometimes feel frustrated with the routines of
cooking, washing, and caring for the children. I
used to wish that I could escape from it all for a
while. Then I came to know Jesus Christ as my

personal Saviour and discovered that He changed my outlook on life and made my work in the home a great joy. I have a few books here which have helped me a lot.'

'Good afternoon. May I take just a moment of your time to show you some books which I have found very helpful in applying the message of the Lord Jesus Christ to my daily life?' (If you receive an affirmative answer, you can move into a lengthier testimony, suiting it to the person and the situation.)

It is not the smoothness with which you rattle off this approach which will make it effective, but the prayer which goes behind it and the sincerity and compassion with which it is used.

4 Children's approach

Often children follow their mother to the door. It is a sure way to the mother's heart if you stop, even in the middle of your sentence, smile at the child and say, 'Hello, how are you today?' To you that child may look like hundreds of other children that you meet, but to the mother her child is one of the most important people in the world. Any attention paid to her child is attention paid to her. You may not honestly be able to say that the child is beautiful (and of course, you should not say anything that is not honest) but you can surely find something to admire or some question to ask indicating interest on your part.

When it is apparent that there are children in the home, you might use one of the following approaches.

'Good morning, madam. I see that you are very busy with your children, and I don't want to take much of your time. I know because of your interest in the welfare of your children that you will want to consider giving them these outstanding children's books . . .'

'Good morning. I know that if you are like many parents you probably do not have much time to read. I have with me some very important books which can be read quickly, and which will help you to have the patience and wisdom you need in bringing up your children.'

When mothers come to the door with a baby in their arms, you can say something like:

'Good afternoon. What a beautiful baby. Do you have other children? It really is a full-time job caring for them, isn't it? It is very important to give children and young people a solid foundation for life, and we have discovered that there is no better foundation than that found in the Bible. I have

with me a selection of Bible story books adapted
for all ages . . .'

5 News item approach

If you are acquainted with local or world news,
some item of general interest can often prove
valuable as a springboard to a sales talk. Make
it a point to read the headlines, giving special
thought to events from which spiritual applications might be drawn. For example:

> 'Good morning, sir. Perhaps you've already read
> in the paper this morning about the peace talks
> our leaders are having. It seems that people are
> constantly speaking of peace, but never able to
> find it. It is a good indication of the desire of
> man's heart to live in peace and security. I have a
> selection of books here which show that real
> heart-peace stems from a right relationship with
> God . . .'

There are many general topics with which you
should be conversant, and which you can use
while speaking to people in their homes. Some
of these are:

● The weather
● Aeroplane crashes or other tragedies
● Wars or humanitarian disasters

- Religious news which hits the secular news media
- Medical discoveries or major events in space exploration

6 The ecumenical approach

Recent developments which are deepening communication between the Roman Catholic and Protestant churches provide increased opportunities to distribute the Scriptures and Christian books in Catholic countries. Many Catholics are much more open to conversation with Protestants than they were. Many Catholic leaders are publicly stating the importance of reading the Bible, and we can use this in speaking with Roman Catholic people.

'Good morning. I presume that you are a Roman Catholic, as are many of my friends. We have many interesting discussions concerning faith in God, and each of them agrees with me that it is important to know what the Bible says. I have with me the whole Bible, as well as portions of it, and also books which explain the message of the Bible.'

'Good morning, sir. One of the issues being discussed much today by Roman Catholic leaders is the importance of the Bible in the church. I am travelling with a group of young people who, during our holidays, are distributing the Scriptures, and I have some copies with me this morning that I am sure you would be interested in.'

7 Local church approach

When we are working with a local church, it is often effective to mention our connection with that church while visiting people in the neighbourhood.

'Good evening, sir. I am from the Emmanuel Bible Church, and we have been visiting different homes to share with people what we believe about the Lord Jesus Christ. If you don't have time to speak with us this evening, we also have with us a small selection of books which explain how each of us can experience God's love and know Him.'

'Good afternoon, John. The young people from our church have been visiting different homes to share with people what the Lord Jesus Christ means to us. He has become our friend, and knowing Him has changed our lives. We've brought along with us a selection of books which have been a real help to us. I think you'll like them, too.'

8 Bible survey approach

You can plan to cover a whole city using this
method, and should be prepared to record the
information gained either in your notebook or
on some sort of card system.

> 'Good afternoon. Our lives have been changed
> through the message of the Bible, and we are car-
> rying out a survey to see what percentage of the
> people in this community read their Bibles. I
> wonder if you would mind taking just a moment
> to answer these questions for me:
>
> Do you have a Bible or a portion of it?
> Do you read it?
> How often do you read it?

For those who answer 'No' to the first question
you can continue:

> 'We have here a Bible as well as a selection of
> good books which explain the message of the
> Bible . . .'

To those who have a Bible but only read it a
little, you might say:

> 'Because of what the Bible has done for me, I
> would like to encourage you to make a practice
> of reading a portion each day. It may be that you

don't read it because you have trouble understanding it. If that is the case, I have some
excellent books here which help to make clear the
truths that are in the Bible.'

9 Special day approach

This approach makes use of any special day to
introduce your books. Any special season or
holiday is usually uppermost in the thoughts of
people and gives you a good opportunity to
'think with them' for just a moment and then
move on to a spiritual application:

'Good morning, madam. I'm sure you are busy
this morning preparing for Christmas. I've come
to wish you a Merry Christmas and to show you
some books which will help you to understand
the real meaning of Christmas. These books are
excellent as gifts . . .'

10 Maid's approach

One problem you might occasionally face in
wealthy areas is what to do when a maid
answers the door. In this situation, salespeople
are quickly turned away. You might immediately ask for the lady of the house, using her
name if you know it:

'Good morning. May I speak to Mrs Radcliffe, please?'

If you do this with confidence the maid, though she may have some question in her mind as to your identity and purpose, may call Mrs Radcliffe, rather than offend an individual who might be a personal friend of her employer.

If the maid does ask your mission, explain to her why you have come, and many times she will call the lady of the house. If she hesitates, do not wait for her to say 'She is busy' or 'She is not here.' Rather, say quickly, 'If she is busy, perhaps you could show her these books.' The lady of the house will seldom come to the door to meet a salesperson, but she may be interested in the books if you can get them to her.

If the maid refuses to show her the books, or if the lady shows no interest in them, do not leave without attempting to sell a Gospel book to the maid. She, of course, is as important in the eyes of the Lord as is the lady of the house.

I hope that these approaches will give you a basis from which to work. You should remember in them all to adapt them to your own situation and your own personality. Ask God to give you perception that you may know which approach to use with an individual. Ask Him to show you what to say, when to say it, and how to say it!

11

Presenting the Books

Having established contact with an individual and introduced the subject of books, you must now move quickly from your general approach to a specific one. This is a strategic point at which you will flounder awkwardly unless you have done some advance planning on how to present your books.

One of the first rules of salesmanship, which is particularly true for house-to-house work, is to know your product. You cannot be sincerely enthusiastic about a book if you are not familiar with its contents. You should also be acquainted with any details which would be good selling points for the book. These could include the number of copies which have been printed, the number of languages into which it has been translated, the renown of the author, the low price of the book, and other such points. Familiarity with these will enable you to develop a sales approach for each book, and this type of approach can be one of the best as the book itself is used as a basis for the conversation.

It is very important while selling to have your books easily accessible, either in your hand or where you can instantly reach them. Then as quickly as possible get the book into the hands of the person you are talking to. The sale will often be made if you can get them leafing through the book.

You are probably asking by now, 'Exactly what books do we sell, and how can we sell them?' These are good questions, and ones I will try to answer in this chapter. The books you choose should be biblically sound in content, moderate in price, and as attractive as possible. You will be limited by the number you can carry, so your selection should include a few basic titles which will meet the needs of the majority of the people you will encounter, including housewives, children, students, businessmen, etc. These will include Bibles and Scripture portions, books on apologetics, Gospel booklets and tracts, children's books, autobiographies and books written specifically for Christians. It is also good, if possible, to have printed lists of books with an address where people can order books at their own convenience.

There are many excellent Christian books published each year in a multitude of languages, and it is difficult to say exactly which books will be best for the situation and country in which you will be working. Often it is best to use books which are written by a national of that country and which effectively present the Gospel, as they can often communicate better to the needs of the people of that country than books which are translated from another language. On the other hand, many books have been translated into a large number of languages and have been influential in changing the lives of hundreds of people in many nations. Although, of course, the actual conversation will not be exactly the same as those given here, I believe that the sample book presentations that are given as a guide in this chapter will be of help to you when you are actually standing at the door wondering, 'What am I going to say about this book?'

1 The Scriptures

The selling of Scriptures is in some ways different from the selling of other books, so it will be covered in the next chapter.

2 Evangelistic books

The main purpose of working door-to-door is to present to people the Gospel of the Lord

Jesus Christ. The books which we want to emphasise are first of all those which clearly present the way of salvation in language that can be understood and appreciated by the average person in the street. Although you may not always begin by offering one of these books, your ultimate goal is to get one into the hands of your contact.

There are excellent Gospel books available in many languages, and we want to mention here some which have been used with great effectiveness throughout the world. The approaches given can of course be adapted to many other books.

a. Peace with God *by Billy Graham*

This is one of the most widely distributed evangelistic books in the world today, and has been translated into many languages. You may want to introduce it by making mention of the renown of the author:

> 'This book, *Peace with God*, was written by Billy Graham. Perhaps you've heard of him? He is a leading Christian spokesman who has spoken personally to more people, including many world leaders than any other man in history. This is his most famous book, and I am sure you will find it really interesting.'

Pointing out the general popularity of the book also helps:

'This book has been translated into more than 35 languages, and hundreds of thousands of copies have been sold around the world. Many people have read it and have found through it the most important thing in life: peace with God! I know that it will help you, too.'

b. The Secret of Happiness, *by Billy Graham*

The title of this book makes it especially appealing to the many who are not interested in religion but who are interested in finding happiness.

'This is an excellent book which answers a question that many people ask: "How can I find true happiness?" We see so few people around us who are truly happy. The message of this book has helped me as well as thousands of other people to experience true happiness.'

It is often a good idea to read through the book and note quotations which would interest a customer in the message of the book:

'This is an interesting book. People today seem to spend an enormous amount of time and money in their search for happiness, but so few find it. In the first chapter of this book, there's the story of a miserable man who visited a psychiatrist and said, "Doctor, I feel so alone and depressed. Can you help me?" The psychiatrist advised him to go to the circus and see a famous clown who was known to make even the most desolate people laugh. The patient replied sadly, "Doctor, I am that clown!" This book goes on to tell how we can find true happiness . . .'

c. Other authors

There are a number of other authors today who have been gifted with the ability to communicate the message of the Gospel and whose books have been translated into many languages and sold by the thousands. The books of Michael Green and David C.K. Watson are written especially for students and young people, and present very clearly the message of the Lord Jesus Christ, as well as the evidences for the truth of that message. Books which present the personal testimonies of those who have come to Christ in an unusual way, like Nicky Cruz, have also been used to bring many to the Lord Jesus. The 'Left Behind' series by Jerry Jenkins and Tim LaHaye has become one of the most popular in the history of church literature, both in Christian and secular bookstores. The sales of other books like *The Prayer of Jabez* have been phenomenal, again in Christian and secular settings. I find that quite a few people do not like these books, but my experience is that the Holy Spirit is using all kinds of books even when they have mistakes and imperfections. You will want to make use of the best books that are available in the language of the country in which you are working.

d. Gospel booklets

These clearly explain the way of salvation and have two distinct advantages in arousing interest. They are inexpensive and they can be read more quickly than a book. There are many excellent booklets which are published today, although perhaps the best known are those published by Jack Chick and also the ones by Life Messengers. They can be obtained at a small cost and have been widely used throughout the world.

e. Gospel comic books

These are also widely distributed today. They present the message of the Gospel in pictorial form. These are excellent for children, but many others find them attractive and you will discover that you can sell a good number of these at the doors.

3 Books on apologetics

Until you begin speaking with a cross-section of people, you will probably never realise how many individuals have intellectual doubts concerning Christianity. Some of these people are hardened sceptics, but many have honest questions which are a hindrance to their becoming Christians.

Some are sceptical only because they have read books presenting arguments for the so-called fallacies of Christianity.

For these people literature is especially valuable. Discussions on such things as the infallibility of the Word of God, the deity of Jesus Christ or the existence of God often accomplish nothing, but a good apologetic book placed in the hands of a sincere person seeking God can accomplish much. The book will not be side-tracked from a calm, logical presentation of the facts of the case, nor will it provoke a heated argument. Books on apologetics are good for almost any thinking person and especially for students.

There are many good books of an apologetic nature which can be sold house-to-house. Books such as *Runaway World* and *Man Alive* by Michael Green are apologetic in nature, while at the same time presenting a clear Gospel message. F.F. Bruce's *The New Testament Documents: Are They Reliable?* is an excellent defence of the accuracy of Scripture, and is invaluable for your own study. The books by Dr Francis Schaeffer, as well as other publications from the L'Abri Fellowship, clearly show the truth of Christianity as well as the veracity of the Bible. C.S. Lewis is another author to be recommended in this area.

Here are some approaches which could be used in presenting a book such as *Basic*

Christianity by John Stott. This book is an investigation of the basic elements of the Christian faith and emphasises particularly the deity of Christ, pointing out the necessity of a personal relationship with Him.

'This is a thought-provoking book, sir. It shows the logic of true Christianity. I don't know what you think of Jesus Christ, but this book helps us to see that He was not only a great man but, as He Himself said many times, the Son of God! This book is not difficult reading, but it does challenge you to think!'

'This book, *Basic Christianity*, is one which approaches Christianity from an intellectual standpoint. It has many chapters giving reasons why we can believe that Jesus Christ was God. This one, for example, on the resurrection, gives logical, historical facts which prove that He did actually arise from the dead. I know in your leisure time you would find it profitable to read this book.'

4 Books for Christians

Although your main purpose in door-to-door work is to reach the unconverted, you will occasionally encounter Christian people in your visits. Many of your books will be excellent to

sell to them, as they can be encouraged to pass
on the Gospel books to unconverted friends,
and books on apologetics are especially good to
help Christians to know why they believe. You
will also want to take with you one or two
books which challenge Christians to a closer
walk with God.

5 Children's books

There are a great variety of children's books
available, and it will be necessary for you to
choose those that you think are best. They should
be chosen on the basis of their attractiveness,
durability, and content. The following ideas may
help you when presenting children's books:

> 'We also have books for children. They love this
> story of David, the little shepherd boy who killed
> a giant. It's a beautiful story, isn't it? And look,
> the cover is washable plastic.'

> 'This is a beautiful book of Bible stories adapted
> for children between the ages of nine and twelve.
> Isn't it important that children have good books
> to read? These are interesting, and also teach the
> importance of obedience and honesty.'

Sometimes in presenting a book, you will want
to avoid the religious angle completely:

'We also have several books for children. Your little girl would love the beautiful pictures in this one, and it has large print and short paragraphs for new readers.'

Children's books are usually the easiest to sell, and sometimes you might want to present them first to gain the attention of your customer. Try to avoid getting only a children's book into the home, as it will not usually contain much of the message of the Gospel. Whenever possible, begin your sales presentation with a Gospel book, as you will often sell the books you actually emphasise. If you do sell a book for the children, follow this up by saying to the parent:

'Your daughter will enjoy this for a long time, I know. Now I have something here that is especially good for you.'

Whenever you only sell a children's book or something that does not present a clear Gospel message, it is important to leave a Gospel booklet or a Gospel as a bonus so the person gets a full presentation of the Gospel.

You must continually keep in mind that in all of these presentations your ultimate goal is to see this person won to Jesus Christ. You do not only want them to buy a book, but you want to do all that you can to encourage them to read it. One good way to do this is to take the book you

have just sold, open it to the table of contents
and point out what one might expect to receive
from the book. If you have just sold *Peace with
God*, you could say:

> 'I'm so glad that you have chosen this book. It is
> one of the very best. I know it will answer many
> questions for you. Mr Graham doesn't only speak
> of the problem of man's lack of peace with God,
> but he also shows the solution. You will want to
> read this chapter on the "New Birth" very care-
> fully. It can bring a real change in your life.'

With a little thought and preparation we can
have Gospel messages ready, prepared on the
contents of each book that we sell! The person
to whom you are speaking will not resent your
testimony if you give it in this way: they will
realise that you are merely passing on to them
ideas of the author which have helped you and
which you feel will be of benefit to others.

Don't feel satisfied just because you have
sold a book! Follow through. Urge that person
to read the book, give a personal testimony
when possible, and challenge them to seek God
with all their heart!

12

Presenting the Scriptures

> 'For the word of God is living and active. Sharper
> than any double-edged sword, it penetrates even
> to dividing soul and spirit, joints and marrow; it
> judges the thoughts and attitudes of the heart'
> (Heb. 4:12).

The Word of God itself is the most powerful
message that we can leave in a home, because it
is His Word which God promises to prosper. In
this chapter we shall consider the distribution
of the Scriptures. In most parts of the world
there is widespread ignorance of the Bible, and
you will meet many people who have only a
vague idea of what the Bible is about. Many
confuse it with the New Testament, prayer
books or missals, and others are surprised to
learn that the four Gospels are in the Bible!
When you are confronted with this ignorance
you will have excellent opportunities, not only
to introduce people to the Scriptures, but also to

---

give direct personal testimony by pointing out verses in the Word itself.

1 The Bible

The following approaches can be used with most individuals:

'This is a copy of the Bible. This is not just an ordinary book, but it is the book which was inspired by God Himself. In this book God reveals Himself to us, and shows us how we can know Him personally.'

'This is a complete Bible. It contains both the Old and New Testaments.' (Many people are ignorant of this fact and while explaining it to them you can show them the general divisions in the Bible itself.)

'Have you a Bible in your home? If not, I'm sure you will be interested in this one. The Pope, as you know, is urging all Roman Catholics to read the Bible, and I have with me both Catholic and Protestant versions. Millions of families throughout the world make it a practice to read the Bible together, and it is well known that this has caused many families to stay closer together.'

'This is a copy of the sacred Scriptures, the Bible. The Bible is a great love story which tells of

God's love for us and how we can experience His love.'

'The Bible will make an ideal gift for your family or friends, and is important for all people. It is something that they want to keep for ever.'

It is a good idea to offer Catholic as well as Protestant versions of the Bible. If you have time, many people will be interested if you compare verses in the Protestant and Catholic versions of the New Testament, and will be surprised to discover that they are basically the same.

The fact that many famous people have felt the Bible to be important influences an individual to purchase a Bible. We have, for example, sold many copies of the New Testament in India by mentioning to people that Mahatma Gandhi stated that he had found much strength and inspiration through the Sermon on the Mount. Comments about the value of the Bible made by well-known people in the country in which you work can encourage many people to buy a copy of the Scriptures for themselves.

Many people buy a Bible with every intention of reading it, then grow discouraged when they begin to read through the Old Testament, or when they just read at random, and find it difficult to understand. It is very important when a complete Bible is sold to take the time to give a few helpful hints about reading it, recommending that they read the Gospel of John first of all, or some other book in the New Testament. If they desire to read the Old Testament, suggest that they read the Psalms or Proverbs and explain to them that they may find the Old Testament difficult to understand without first reading the New.

2 The New Testament

The New Testament is generally not difficult to sell, as it is relatively inexpensive and most people who know it acknowledge its importance. Many Christians prefer to sell the New Testament rather than the complete Bible, especially to the unconverted. Here are a few suggestions for presenting it:

'This is the New Testament, which is the second part of the Bible. It gives the life and teachings of Jesus and explains how we can experience God's love and receive His salvation.'

'This little book, the New Testament, has changed more lives than any other book in existence. I find that reading from it each day gives me strength and help in my life. I recommend that you begin your reading of the New Testament here in the Gospel of John. It is the easiest to understand.'

While presenting the New Testament you also have an open door to clearly present the Gospel. One of the best ways to do this, even if you don't speak the language of the person, is simply to point out some of the key verses of the New Testament. This will arouse interest in the book as well as giving a better idea of its contents.

3 Single Gospels and other Scripture portions

There will be times when you will have had the opportunity to share your testimony or present the Gospel to a person, and you will simply want to give them a Gospel of John or another portion of Scripture as a gift, rather than charging them for it. At other times, you will find that the person will appreciate the Gospel more if they pay a small price for it. In either case, it is always good to give the person some reasons why they should read the Gospel, for it will mean relatively little if they take it but never read it.

Distribution of Gospels is important in any area, but is particularly worthwhile in poor areas as they can be offered at a very low price. They are one of the easiest items to sell from house to house or where crowds are gathered, and many young people who find selling books very difficult have great success in selling Gospels of John. What could be better to leave in homes than the biblical account of the life and teachings of Jesus?

One of the most effective means of distributing Gospels is simply by holding out the Gospel on the street saying something like this:

'Sir, would you like a copy of one of the world's most widely read books? It only costs . . .'

'Have you read this amazing little book? It contains the most important message we were ever given, and it only costs . . .'

Many times a Gospel of John can be used as a premium to stimulate interest in a larger book. You might say, for example, 'This Gospel of John is free if you purchase another book.'

You will meet many people who will tell you that the message of the Bible is irrelevant for our times, or who will speak of the alleged contradictions of Scripture. It is best not to argue with them, especially if you are not able to answer all of the questions that they raise. Many times it is more effective to say in a few words how the Lord Jesus Christ has changed your life, and to ask them if they have really examined the evidence for the authority of the Bible. Many have not done so, and the objections that they raise can be turned into opportunities to sell books which present the basis for our faith in Christ and the Word of God.

There are many books available which show clearly that the Bible is without error, and truly is the Word of God. It is very important to study some of these, for you need to be able to give reasons for your trust in the Bible. It will take time and study on your part to become familiar with this most important subject, but it will be a great weapon in reaching people for Christ. It is always important, when we speak of the Bible, to state with conviction that we do believe it to be the Word of God.

Because so many people are so ignorant about the Bible, it is always wise when you sell any part of the Scriptures to follow through with one or all of the following steps:

1. Explain what the Scriptures are.
2. Give practical suggestions about how to read them, encouraging the person to begin with the portions that you think would be most beneficial, and encouraging them to read some each day.
3. Offer books which will help to explain the Scriptures.
4. Give the person an address to which they can write for a free correspondence course enabling them to study the Bible in their own home.

Modern translations of the Bible are now being published in many countries around the world, and the opportunities to present these to people are inexhaustible. I hope that the few comments in this chapter will help you to distribute many copies of God's Word to those with no real knowledge or understanding of it.

13

Literature and the Local Church

All evangelism should be aimed primarily at presenting the Gospel to lost men and women, and bringing them into a personal relationship with the Lord Jesus Christ. The goal must then be to establish them into local groups of believers – churches. It is imperative in our literature evangelism to keep this ultimate end uppermost in our minds and to do all we can to make this become a reality so that our work will not be without lasting significance.

This means that any literature evangelism programme should be carried out in co-operation with local evangelical churches. If in your area no such churches exist, the goal of your work should be to establish them. It may not always be possible for you to engage in the actual work of starting a church, but this does not lessen your responsibility to contribute to its establishment. This could involve asking other missionaries or Christian workers to come and continue the work you have begun. It might mean passing on your contacts to the nearest evangelical church, whose members could plant a church in the area in which you have been working.

On the other hand, each church should realise that effectiveness can be greatly increased by making full use of Christian literature and other communication tools. Most growing churches use such tools extensively, and acknowledge their role in the development of the church. This chapter lists only a few of many ways that any church can increase its effectiveness through literature.

1 Door-to-door visiting

Each church should have a systematic programme for door-to-door visiting. Most people will never come of their own volition to hear the Gospel: it is personal interest shown in them by believers that will bring them from their homes. Literature used in visiting greatly increases the possibility of a permanent impact. The message given verbally can be reinforced by the pamphlet left in the home, together with an invitation to visit the church.

Some churches use a 'census', through which they obtain general religious information from the people whom they visit. The initial visits are usually brief, but prepare the way for future visits. Here again it is important to leave some literature behind, saying simply, 'I hope that we can have a longer talk someday. Could I leave this with you to read in your spare time?'

If you can let people know in advance that you would like to visit them, they can set a definite time when they will be at home. When you visit them, take several books and tracts which you think will meet their needs. It is sometimes very effective to lend a salvation book, telling the people that you will come back to collect the book in a week or two. This not only encourages them to read the book, but also gives you another opportunity to return and develop your friendship.

2 Printed invitations

Many churches print small cards or pamphlets inviting people to attend their services. These usually include the times of the services, and sometimes a brief statement of the basic doctrines of the church or a short presentation of the Gospel. A supply of these should be available for each member of the congregation to distribute to friends and neighbours, and should also be included in the regular visiting programme.

3 Printed sermons or message cassettes

Some churches record their minister's best sermons and print these in pamphlet form. They can then be distributed to those who are unable to attend the church, such as those who are housebound, servicemen and women, and young people who are away at college. Some churches also carry programmes on local radio stations, and sermon tapes are made available to all listeners who request them. CDs are also now being used effectively in a similar way.

4 Tract racks

A good selection of Gospel tracts, attractively displayed in a convenient part of the church building, encourages visitors to help themselves, and reminds members to take large quantities for distribution. The church address or web site is sometimes stamped on the reverse side of the tract. This can be a disadvantage in some countries, as many people will not read a tract that has a religious address on it. It is sometimes better if the address used does not reveal its religious character – a box number, for example. Each church must decide what is best for its particular situation.

5 Book tables

Some churches have set up a book table with books and other materials suitable both for Christians and non-Christians. If there are some who object to selling books within the church building, a box can be placed on the table in which donations can be given to cover the cost of the books. Such a table may be permanent, or it may be set up only during special meetings. To whatever extent it is used, it can have a vital part in contributing to the growth of Christians, especially in an area where no Christian bookshop exists. Many Christian bookshops are willing to supply books for church book tables at a small discount under a book-agency scheme. The small profit made covers costs, dead stock, etc.

6 Lending Libraries

Rather than selling books, some churches prefer to have a lending library from which books and other items can be borrowed for a specific period of time. Other churches have a library as well as a book table, as there are always some books that people would like to keep permanently and others that they would prefer just to read and return.

Many church libraries unfortunately seem to be in such inconspicuous corners that the majority of the people don't even know they exist. They should be placed so that people will be constantly reminded that they are there. New books should be added periodically, and the covers could be displayed on the church bulletin board. It is very important that a responsible person with concern for this ministry be put in charge of the library and that books in it be frequently brought to the attention of the church members. It takes constant encouragement to develop a 'reading' congregation.

7 Correspondence courses

Correspondence courses can provide one of the most effective ways to bring people into contact with the local church. Missionaries throughout the world realise this and there is now a great tendency to print tracts with an emphasis on follow-up. This might be in the form of a coupon which can be clipped off and sent in. It might be in the form of a postcard. Or it might be simply printing an address to which people can write to request a Bible correspondence course. The first two are preferable.

All those who respond are sent a correspondence course, one lesson at a time. Many correspondence-course officials will refer the names of their students to the local church which ideally should visit and sometimes help them in their study of the Bible. In Europe many churches distribute tracts, receive names and addresses, and follow these up. Many have been brought into fellowship with Christ and His church in this manner.

8 Letters

One of the greatest ministries of the apostle Paul was letter-writing. It can be vital for Christians today as well, but sadly often seems to be neglected. We are 'too busy' to write letters, we 'don't like' to write them, or we are simply unaware of their effectiveness. Self-discipline is the key to an effective ministry in this area. Many times a personal letter can have more effect than an actual conversation. One thing you can be sure of is that a personal letter is always read! By sitting down and applying yourself you can think of dozens of people who would be happy to receive a letter from you. These letters need not be long, but in them you can present in a friendly, tactful way what Jesus Christ means to you and include, along with the letter, an interesting tract. You will find that through correspondence you can deepen friendships with many people and you can also be used to help them in problems that they face in their lives.

9 Book reviews

There are innumerable Christian books available, but the problem is that many Christians just don't read them. One good way to overcome this is to arrange a challenging talk by someone in the church on the need to study the Word of God and to read Christian books: this talk can emphasise that reading helps us to understand our own faith more adequately and be better prepared to present this faith to other people.

Book reviews provide another excellent way to stimulate reading. They can be given at a special meeting, or as part of one of the weekly services. In a few minutes a short challenge can be given on the contents of a particular book, with reasons why it should be read. Preparation and enthusiasm on the part of the reviewer are essential: if it is to accomplish its purpose the review must be so interesting that people will be moved to read the book. Needless to say, the book should be available for them to read!

To summarise, literature and other communication tools can be one of the most effective instruments for advancing the growth of the local church and for building up Christians in their faith. Over the past 40 years we have seen the explosion of cell churches and all kinds of small group activity. Literature and other communication tools have played a vital role in this. It is very important that interdenominational organisations remember that God's main means of spreading the Gospel here on earth is through each individual member of the church. All activities should be engaged upon with this in mind so that God's plan can be accomplished in this way.

At the same time local churches need to realise the tremendous potential of Christian literature, and they should co-operate as much as possible with the various literature ministries that are being carried on in their own countries. A closer union between these two groups could enable millions of people to be reached with the Gospel of Christ, leading to the establishment of many more local churches, as well as the strengthening of existing ones.

14

Watering the Seed

We can never be satisfied in evangelism with simply sowing the seed. We must constantly desire that fruit should spring forth and multiply. This means that one of the most vital parts of true literature evangelism is watering the seed by prayer.

The prayer-life of the Lord Jesus Christ stands out in the Gospels as our greatest example of prayer. The apostle Paul is remembered for such sayings as 'Pray without ceasing' and what we read of his life bears testimony to the fact that he practised what he preached. Every servant of God of whom we read in the Scriptures, as well as every servant of God throughout history, has been a person of prayer!

Often our concept of prayer is merely that of asking and receiving. However, praise, thanksgiving and worship cannot be separated from true evangelism. The world can only be evangelised as the fruit of our intimate relationship with the living God. If we desire with all our hearts to see the world reached for Christ, and if we long to see a harvest of souls, we must learn to walk and talk with God. We must, like every true disciple, sit at the feet of our Master and learn what it is to live a life of prayer.

Prayer is the weapon which God has given us to tear down the strongholds of the enemy. We read in 2 Corinthians 10:4 that 'the weapons we fight with are not the weapons of the world. On the contrary, they have divine power to demolish strongholds'. Unfortunately, few of God's children seem to realise that there is a war raging. Imagine what would happen if each Christian began to live as a soldier in accordance with what Paul said in 2 Timothy 2:4, 'No-one serving as a soldier gets involved in civilian affairs – he wants to please his commanding officer.' Can you imagine what would happen if Christians would, as this verse teaches, live unentangled lives, giving themselves to the spiritual warfare at hand? It is only by grasping and using the weapon of prayer that strongholds of Satan will be torn down and the Gospel will bring forth fruit.

We must turn again to the Acts of the Apostles and see that it was when the early church prayed that God moved and souls were saved. We must confess that we do not understand prayer. We cannot fully explain it or describe its many theological implications. Yet we know that it works! Prayer worked in the days of Abraham, Moses, and Elijah; it worked in the time of Peter and Paul; and it worked during the lives of George Muller, John Wesley and Hudson Taylor. It also works today! Unless we learn to pray, we will never see much fruit in our evangelism no matter how many millions of tracts we distribute, no matter how many thousands of books we sell, and no matter how many testimonies we give or sermons we preach!

By God's grace, we must learn to meet Him in private prayer. We must learn to pray together in groups. We must take the maps of cities, provinces, and countries, of the whole world and agonise in believing prayer. It is then that the fruit of evangelism will come forth:

'Those who sow in tears will reap with songs of joy . . . He who goes out weeping, carrying seed to say, will return with songs of joy, carrying sheaves with him' (Ps. 126:5,6).

Only God brings forth the fruit, but He does so in response to desperate, believing prayer on the part of His people. Oh, that we may be clean channels so that God can use us for this vital task of watering the seed by prayer! Only this will bring about world evangelism. The task is in itself impossible, and will never be accomplished except through 'prayer and fasting'. This is a huge burden on our hearts. I hope many will check out my web site georgeverwer.com to read what I have to say. My leaflet, *What Happened to the Prayer Meeting* has also gone around the world in many languages.

15

The Greatest Need

How easily our evangelistic work will become nothing more than a 'resounding gong or a clanging cymbal' if we fail to carry it out in accordance with Christ's greatest commandments: '"Love the Lord your God with all your heart and with all your soul and with all your mind." This is the first and greatest commandment. And the second is like it: "Love your neighbour as yourself"' (Mt. 22:37–9). Many can testify that obedience to these verses has changed their lives. If we meditate upon them and take them seriously, our lives can also be transformed, and we will be motivated to commit ourselves to reaching our neighbours with the Gospel of Jesus Christ.

Jesus taught in the Parable of the Good Samaritan that loving our neighbours involves willingly giving that which we have to help those who are in need. If we meditate upon this, and realise that the second great commandment is to love our neighbour as we love ourselves, we will find dynamic teaching which is so radical that obedience to it would lead to a spiritual revolution that would turn the world upside down as in the early years of the Christian church.

Love must be our supreme motive for involvement in evangelism. Without love we can seemingly accomplish much, but it will mean nothing. We read in Matthew 9:35 that 'Jesus went through all the towns and villages, teaching in their synagogues, preaching the good news of the kingdom and healing every disease and sickness.' In the very next verse, we see His motive for doing this: 'When he saw the crowds, he had compassion on them, because they were harassed and helpless, like sheep without a shepherd.' It must be the same with us in our literature evangelism. We must be moved with compassion and, as Paul said, be compelled by the love of Christ. This means that we must learn to live each moment in Him, allowing Him to take complete control of all we do and all we think. As we do this, we will find ourselves moving out in evangelism as Jesus did when He was here on the earth. Our motive will be compassion – His love expressed through us.

What has been mere theory to many of us must become real, a daily practice in our lives. Without this love, all that we do will amount to

The Greatest Need   121

nothing more than noise, and although people may be temporarily impressed, God will know that we are running in vain and only beating the air. It must be the love of Christ that motivates us. We must, at whatever cost, learn the reality of verses such as Philippians 2:3: 'Do nothing out of selfish ambition or vain conceit, but in humility consider others better than yourselves. Each of you should look not only to your own interests, but also to the interests of others.' It is not enough merely to talk about having been crucified with Christ, but we must learn to take up our cross each day and follow Him. The world can only be reached as we identify ourselves totally with the sufferings, death, and resurrection of the Lord Jesus Christ. This, without any doubt, is our greatest need.

This concept is expressed in many ways in the Scriptures, and is talked about by large numbers of Christians. It can basically be summed up in the words, 'Not I, but Christ.' Not my will, but His! Not my way, but His! Not my love, but His! Not my life, but His! When this need is met in our lives, and only then, we will experience God's blessing in our efforts to reach every person with the Gospel of Christ.

It is still true that over half the total population of the world has never in any form received the message of the Gospel of Jesus Christ. Whether they ever do hear will depend entirely on our reaction to the message of this chapter. It is the basic message of the New Testament, and can be summarised by 1 John 3:16: 'This is how we know what love is: Jesus Christ laid down his life for us. And we ought to lay down our lives for our brothers.'

It was the love of God which sent Jesus to this earth to die on the cross for our sins, and it is this same love which must send us to the cross to be made dead to sin! As we die to ourselves, we are made alive to God and become motivated by His love, so that in the power of the Holy Spirit we can be His witnesses to the Gospel even to the ends of the earth.

The millions without the Gospel can and will hear, if we are willing to take God at His Word and allow Christ to take complete control of our lives so that everything we say and do will be motivated by love and compassion. There is no other way. All that has been written in this book will be of absolutely no value if we are not willing to 'fall into the ground and die' so that He might live in us and bring forth much fruit – fruit that will remain!

What I speak of in this chapter is the basis for all my other books that have gone out around the globe and I hope you will read some of them. Hundreds of different message tapes and videos are also available. Don't hesitate to contact us for a list of them.

ISBN 1-85078-353-5

Reading this book could seriously change your attitude! George Verwer doesn't pull any punches in his heart's cry for a 'grace-awakened' approach to mission. His approach is down-to-earth, honest and thoroughly biblical. After 40 years experience in mission, he is still learning and open to change – and he expects no less of you, the reader. George Verwer is known throughout the world as a motivator and mobiliser. *Out of the Comfort Zone* should only be read by those who are willing to accept God's grace, catch His vision and respond with action in the world of mission.

OM publishing

ISBN 0-85364-949-9

Leadership is a key to success in any organisation.
All the more reason to get it right, says Viv Thomas
in a book that sets out to discern the kind of
leadership that is needed in the new millennium.
Driven by compassion, not obsession – rooted in
relationships, not systems – promotes life, not self-
image. This stimulating and inspiring book will test
all that might aspire to lead. Viv Thomas is the
International Co-ordinator of Leadership Development with Operation Mobilisation. He is also a
visiting lecturer at All Nations Christian College in
Hertfordshire.

paternoster
press